Advance Praise for
Knowing Our Worth

Knowing Our Worth is a charming discussion between a German environmental scientist and a Japanese Buddhist thinker. While recognizing the importance of resource and energy efficiency, the authors perceive that economic ideas of efficiency are not enough to counter the logic of financial selfishness. They call for a human revolution that would move us toward a world without war, a world in which ideas of growth are subordinate to ethical and practical ideas of frugality and sustainability in a context of social justice. They propose an Asian-European alliance toward a "new enlightenment" that would combine the ideas from science and religion that are most critical for humanity today and in the future.
> —Neva Goodwin, Co-director, Global Development and
> Environment Institute, Tufts University

Taking ourselves off the self-endangered species list requires a human revolution—a transformation of what we do and why, as we strive to become better human beings in more compassionate and durable societies. Drawing from great Asian and European civilizations, this book distills valuable and practical insights on sufficiency through efficiency, simplicity, public purpose, and civic responsibility.
> —Amory B. Lovins, Cofounder and Chief Scientist, Rocky
> Mountain Institute; coauthor, *Factor Four* and *Natural Capitalism*

This wonderful dialogue between Daisaku Ikeda and Ernst Ulrich von Weizsäcker embraces the emergence of planetary awareness among citizens worldwide. Today's sense of urgency arises from witnessing global environmental destruction resulting from limited human consciousness and consequent human despair—evidenced in dysfunctional policies, illness, depression, addiction, violence, and terrorism.

The authors remind me of modern bodhisattvas: facing humanity's current challenges with hope, deep analyses, research, and dedicated compassionate action. Both these hardy souls engage with the most important global issues, shaping new paradigms, debates, and policies for our common future.

Knowing Our Worth will remain a valuable guide to rising generations of global citizens in all countries as they join together to create humane societies beyond market fundamentalism, GDP-fetishism, commercialism, and mindless consumption.

—Hazel Henderson, President, Ethical Markets Media;
author, *Mapping the Global Transition to the Solar Age*

Knowing Our Worth

Knowing Our Worth

Conversations on Energy and Sustainability

ERNST ULRICH VON WEIZSÄCKER

DAISAKU IKEDA

Dialogue Path Press
Cambridge, Massachusetts
2016

Published by Dialogue Path Press
Ikeda Center for Peace, Learning, and Dialogue
396 Harvard Street
Cambridge, Massachusetts 02138

Cover design by Gopa & Ted2, Inc.
Interior design by Gopa & Ted2, Inc., and Eric Edstam

ISBN: 978-1-887917-15-5

Library of Congress Cataloging-in-Publication Data

Names: Weizsèacker, Ernst U. von (Ernst Ulrich), 1939- author. | Ikeda, Daisaku,
    author.
Title: Knowing our worth : conversations on energy and sustainability / Ernst Ulrich
    Von Weizsèacker, Daisaku Ikeda.
Description: Cambridge, Mass. : Dialogue Path Press, 2015. | Includes bibliographical
    references and index.
Identifiers: LCCN 2015050903 | ISBN 9781887917155 (pbk. : alk. paper)
Subjects: LCSH: Sustainable development. | Environmentalism.
Classification: LCC HC79.E5 W4525 2015 | DDC 338.9/27--dc23
LC record available at http://lccn.loc.gov/2015050903

10 9 8 7 6 5 4 3 2 1

About Dialogue Path Press

Dialogue Path Press is the publishing arm of the Ikeda Center for Peace, Learning, and Dialogue, and is dedicated to publishing titles that foster cross-cultural dialogue and greater human flourishing. Books published by the Center (including those produced in collaboration with other publishers before the establishment of Dialogue Path Press) have been used in more than 900 college and university courses. Previous titles are:

Our World To Make: Hinduism, Buddhism, and the Rise of Global Civil Society (2015)

Living As Learning: John Dewey in the 21st Century (2014)

The Art of True Relations: Conversations on the Poetic Heart of Human Possibility (2014)

America Will Be!: Conversations on Hope, Freedom, and Democracy (2013)

The Inner Philosopher: Conversations on Philosophy's Transformative Power (2012)

Into Full Flower: Making Peace Cultures Happen (2010)

Creating Waldens: An East-West Conversation on the American Renaissance (2009)

About the Ikeda Center

The Ikeda Center for Peace, Learning, and Dialogue is a nonprofit institution founded by Buddhist thinker and leader Daisaku Ikeda in 1993. Located in Cambridge, Massachusetts, the Center engages diverse scholars, activists, and social innovators in the search for the ideas and solutions that will assist in the peaceful evolution of humanity. Ikeda Center programs include public forums and scholarly seminars that are organized collaboratively and offer a range of perspectives on key issues in global ethics. The Center was initially called the Boston Research Center for the 21st Century and became the Ikeda Center in 2009.

For more information, visit the Ikeda Center website: www.ikedacenter.org

Table of Contents

Ernst Ulrich von Weizsäcker (right) and Daisaku Ikeda

CONVERSATION ONE

Hope and Recovery

IKEDA: Dialogue is an expression of our humanity. Dialogue is a communion of souls and a light illuminating the future. I am very happy to have this opportunity to engage in dialogue with you, Dr. Weizsäcker.

You are one of the world's leading scholars of environmental studies, and you have offered many concrete proposals for protecting the environment and taken action to create a sustainable society. There is much I can learn from you. Our dialogue, I hope, will make a positive contribution to the future of our planet and to the peace of humankind.

WEIZSÄCKER: I consider it an honor to engage in this dialogue with you, President Ikeda of the Soka Gakkai International. Thank you for the opportunity.

You speak of wishing to make a contribution to the future of our planet and to the peace of humankind; in fact, anyone who cares about peace cannot help but direct their gaze toward Buddhism.

The Soka Gakkai's vital tradition of acting for peace—which can be traced back to your movement's founder, the first president,

Tsunesaburo Makiguchi, and his struggle against militarism in World War II—deserves recognition from us in Europe and also from our friends in America.

IKEDA: Thank you. As you note, our movement's starting point is President Makiguchi's struggle for peace and humanism. Firmly upholding the Buddhist philosophy of the dignity of life, he took courageous action for the people's happiness and, in his struggle with the militarist authorities that governed Japan at the time, died for his beliefs in prison.[1] The year 2011,[2] in fact, marks the 140th anniversary of his birth. President Makiguchi was an outstanding geographer,[3] calling for the symbiosis of human beings and their environment. I am sure he would be happy about this dialogue with you, a leading environmentalist.

You attended the graduation ceremony for Soka University and Soka Women's College in March 2010.[4] Our students were deeply impressed and inspired by your efforts to build a network for goodness as you travel around the world speaking. The students whose graduation you helped to celebrate are now all engaged in their own careers in Japan and around the world, committed to their personal missions to make the world a better place.

WEIZSÄCKER: Yes, that was our first meeting. I was moved by your warm, fatherly concern for the students. I recall you told the students at their graduation ceremony to have courage and to do their best as they went out into the world. I am glad to hear that they are all doing well with the spirit they learned at Soka University. I had read your peace proposals[5] in the past, but upon meeting you in person, I was especially impressed by your concern for youth. I also noted your expressions of concern and appreciation for the students' parents, who had made it possible for them to attend university and college.

I was struck, too, by how you urged the faculty to care for the students as if they were their own children. As you said, when a faculty has this attitude toward students, the university and college are certain to flourish.

The Tragedy of March 2011

IKEDA: Young people are our greatest treasure. I believe our dialogue on environmental issues will be deeply significant for the young people to whom we cannot help but entrust our planet's future.

Let me take this opportunity to thank you once again for the message of condolence and warm encouragement that you sent immediately following the devastating earthquake and tsunami that struck Japan's Tohoku region in March 2011.[6] There were too many precious lives lost. In the wake of this natural disaster of unprecedented proportions, many have had to live in evacuation shelters. Those from the damaged areas are doing their best to move forward day by day, in the face of indescribable challenges and sufferings.

Together with many others, we of the Soka Gakkai have been fully engaged in relief and rebuilding efforts since the day of the first quake, March 11, but the obstacles to any return to normality are enormous. Many are facing the grief of losing their family members, loved ones, and their livelihoods in one instantaneous stroke; they face uncertain futures, and prospects for economic recovery are lagging.

Yet I know of many remarkable individuals who, though they themselves lost family members and homes in the tsunami, are earnestly engaged in helping others. One can't help but be deeply moved and impressed by the noble humanitarian efforts of many local people in the face of this horrific event. To me, they stand as shining beacons of hope. We of the Soka Gakkai are determined to redouble our efforts to aid and support the victims[7] at this time, calling for mutual support and encouragement and a strong net-work of people helping one another.

At the same time, the series of nuclear accidents at the Fuku-shima Prefecture reactors following the earthquake and tsunami are extremely serious threats.[8] The spread of the resulting radiation contamination, which is of course invisible to the eye, has been deeply unsettling to those in the directly affected areas and the Japanese people as a whole. Resolving the nuclear accidents and aiding those affected are urgent concerns. These events force us to rethink, from the foundation up, the assumptions upon which modern civilization rests.

WEIZSÄCKER: Please let me repeat my sincerest condolences to all who have been affected by the March 2011 earthquake, tsunami, and subsequent nuclear accidents. It was a disaster of enormous proportions, not only for those directly affected but for the Japa-nese people as a whole.

I sincerely believe, however, that the process of overcoming the tragedy can serve as an opportunity for the growth of a new and better civilization. I hope that the Japanese people will recapture the spirit of dynamism and optimism that they demonstrated to the world in the 1970s and 1980s. I hope they will rouse their courage and lead the way in the construction of a society based on environmental protection—an issue of international concern in the twenty-first century—and free from dependence on nuclear energy, creating a groundswell of technological innovation.

I look to Japan to build a new civilization based not on environ-mental destruction but on environmental protection. I am fully aware that Japan's heavy dependence in every respect on nuclear energy is the result of a long series of circumstances and events, but I also believe that the Japanese people can, through their intel-ligence and innovative skills, develop efficient new technologies before both Europe and the United States.

The experience of World War II taught both Germany and Japan the painful lesson of the importance of building a peaceful world. We survived that trial, and I hope and firmly believe that the Japanese people can survive this one as well and rise up again with renewed hope and optimism.

IKEDA: I am deeply impressed by your words of the most profound friendship and trust.

Immediately after the earthquake, German President Christian Wulff and Chancellor Angela Merkel visited the Japanese Embassy in Berlin to offer their condolences and called on the German people to make donations to the victims. In addition, the German Federal Agency for Technical Relief (Bundesanstalt Technisches Hilfswerk, or THW) provided support to search for and rescue survivors, and Germany extended a helping hand in many other ways. Let me take this opportunity to express our deepest appreciation.

We, the Japanese people, were greatly encouraged by the numerous forms of support and aid given us by Germany and many other countries. No matter how far away they lived, people around the world shared the pain of our tragedy and reached out to us. This spirit of care and concern played a major role in recovery efforts.

Because of the scale of the destruction, the road to recovery will, no doubt, be long and perilous, but as you say, Japan has recovered in the past from the tragedy of the nuclear attacks on Hiroshima and Nagasaki, which were so devastating that many thought no life could ever return to those sites. I firmly believe that we human beings possess the power of hope and recovery, which allows us to encourage one another and take new steps forward, though we may encounter difficulties and hardships.

In the past, I met with the renowned economist John Kenneth Galbraith, who, commenting on Japan's recovery from the devastation of World War II, said that it is the people who drive the economy. He firmly believed that if the people of a society have the will, they can overcome the harshest circumstances or direst adversities and become the counterforce for recovery, restoration, and renewed growth, leading their society to prosperity.

Though Dr. Galbraith was speaking mainly of economic recovery, I think this idea applies to society in general. The restoration of the human spirit is a force leading to the revival of communities and the recovery of society as a whole.

Nichiren, the Japanese Buddhist thinker and reformer whose teachings we of the SGI uphold and practice, said, "When great evil occurs, great good follows."[9] The Japanese people are working together to face this calamity and achieve a sound recovery, taking this as a turning point leading to great advancement.

THE LIMITS TO GROWTH

WEIZSÄCKER: The German people felt tremendous sympathy for the victims of the earthquake and tsunami and the subsequent nuclear accidents. We immediately asked ourselves how it would feel if a similar series of events were to occur in Germany or France. As a result, the German government halted the extension to the longevity of the country's nuclear power stations.[10]

The accidents at the Fukushima power plants, while having no direct bearing on the safety of German nuclear power plants, triggered an outburst of the underlying anxiety the German people felt about nuclear power, and public opinion suddenly shifted in support of ending nuclear power generation. This was true across the political spectrum—not only the Green Party and the Social Democratic Party of Germany, which had for more than twenty years opposed nuclear power, but also within the Christian Democratic Union and the Free Democratic Party.

The argument no longer focused on the advantages and shortcomings of coal-fired energy plants, wind power, and nuclear power. Instead, it shifted to a serious effort to improve energy efficiency. In other words, the need for a dramatic improvement in energy efficiency finally became a political issue.

IKEDA: We in Japan have been following the developments in Germany with great interest. Energy is an extremely urgent problem—not just in terms of economic growth but as an inseparable factor in the environmental problems we face and, as you said earlier, in considering how to create a new civilization based on new values, a new perspective on society.

I published the dialogue *Before It Is Too Late* with Aurelio Peccei, a cofounder of the Club of Rome, in 1984. It turned out to be one of Dr. Peccei's final publications. In it, I pointed out the many problematic aspects of dependence on nuclear power and concluded that it should not be regarded as our main source of energy, replacing dwindling supplies of petroleum.

Energy efficiency is one of your areas of specialization. You said in an interview that

> humanity's scientific advances up to now were all focused on expansion. In this century, however, their focus must shift to sustainability. We need to learn to re-metabolize smaller amounts of energy for our wealth and happiness.[11]

I agree with you. Your new book, *Factor Five: Transforming the Global Economy through 80% Improvements in Resource Productivity*, which you gave me as a gift, presents concrete ways to achieve this.

WEIZSÄCKER: In *Factor Five*, my Australian co-authors and I show that a fivefold increase in resource productivity is possible. This allows more growth for the poor countries without more resource consumption while demonstrating to the rich countries that they can reduce their resource consumption fivefold without jeopardizing their economic well-being.

I read your dialogue with Dr. Peccei. I do recall being impressed that both of you definitely possessed a global outlook, offered a perceptive critique of the forces that control and animate the world of today, and emphasized our need to take responsibility for our actions.

The Earth is big and amazingly robust. Unfortunately, much of it is being destroyed at the moment; but there are also signs of its capacity for regeneration. If, as I describe in *Factor Five,* we succeed in stabilizing the population and manage to develop technology in a way that the pressure on nature per unit of well-being is reduced by a minimum of Factor Five—and some day by a Factor Twenty—then we do have a chance indeed.

IKEDA: You offer a grand, pioneering vision and an important change in our way of conceptualizing and formulating the issue.

I think that the characteristic tendency of contemporary civilization can be summed up as the pursuit of wealth through the consumption of enormous quantities of natural resources. The idea of Factor Five suggests that huge amounts of resource consumption are not essential for producing wealth. This is an entirely new way of thinking about the issue, which is what has drawn me to your approach.

Dr. Peccei said, "New guidelines for our thinking and action are indispensable if we are to march safely and serenely into the future."[12] I am certain that your ideas will serve as an extremely important guidepost for humanity's future. Looking back, the report of the Club of Rome, *The Limits to Growth,* in 1972, was first to declare that there are limits to a society founded on the notion of unchecked economic expansion, and that the paradigm underlying the culture of rampant consumerism needs to be transformed.

WEIZSÄCKER: *The Limits to Growth* was an outcry. Using a computer model representing temporal interactions between a small number of major parameters, it showed in dramatic terms that the coupled world system of population growth, industrial growth, farming, pollution, and resource consumption would lead to collapse both in terms of pollution and resource depletion.

On the other hand, some of the mathematical assumptions were wrong, notably the rigid coupling between industrial outputs and pollution. Fortunately for humankind, the age of pollution control became a success story at about the time of the publication of *The Limits to Growth*. Now is the time to provide positive answers to the challenges highlighted in *The Limits to Growth*.

Pollution was the big calamity of the 1960s. Protests against local pollution sparked citizens' movements in many countries, including Germany. In 1969, when I began working for the Protestant interdisciplinary think tank FEST (Forschungsstätte der Evangelischen Studiengemeinschaft), directed by Professor Georg Picht, environmental policy was already on my agenda. In a research group I coordinated, we explored ways and means of using good science to help overcome the environmental crisis. We were among the first in Germany to notice the Club of Rome project "The Predicament of Mankind" from which *The Limits to Growth* emerged. When I was appointed professor of biology at the University of Essen (at the time separate from the University of Duisburg), it was absolutely plausible to engage in environmental studies, and our team at Essen designed and later established the equivalent of a graduate course in environmental science and planning, one of the earliest in Germany.

IKEDA: You already shared a common awareness of these issues with the Club of Rome, didn't you? I understand that Professor Picht was a close friend of your father, Dr. Carl Friedrich von Weizsäcker, and was one of the first to recognize the importance of the Club of Rome's *Limits to Growth*. Later, I want to ask you more about Professor Picht, with whom you formed a profound friendship.

I was fortunate to make the acquaintance of Dr. Peccei while the controversy stirred by *The Limits to Growth* was still very alive in people's minds. As a matter of fact, we met through the British historian Arnold J. Toynbee, with whom I spent about forty hours in 1972 and 1973 engaging in dialogue at his London home. When we finished, he handed me a note containing the names of several intellectuals, saying, "These are some of my friends." Dr. Toynbee urged me to contact them if I had the opportunity and engage in dialogues with them, and Dr. Peccei was on the list.

In retrospect, it strikes me as serendipitous that *The Limits to Growth* was published just when I was discussing environmental issues with Dr. Toynbee. The Dutch journalist Willem L. Oltmans, with the cooperation of Dr. Peccei, reported on the reaction to the report around the world. Mr. Oltmans interviewed Dr. Toynbee right after my first meeting with the historian, and he was also one of those named in Dr. Toynbee's list, though I unfortunately never had the opportunity to meet him.

The Limits to Growth expressed in clear, unmistakable language the threats posed to the survival of our planet not only by nuclear war but also by the depletion of natural resources and environmental destruction. In 1975, as global awareness of the threat to our survival as a species and planet was spreading worldwide, I encountered Dr. Peccei and the Club of Rome. Later, I also published a dialogue with the Club's honorary president Ricardo Díez-Hochleitner. My friendship with the Club of Rome has continued now for many years.

In a way, I regard my present dialogue with you as a continuation of my friendship with the Club of Rome members and the third volume in a series of dialogues with them, starting with *Before It Is Too Late* with Dr. Peccei and followed by *A Dialogue Between East and West: Looking to a Human Revolution* with Dr. Díez-Hochleitner.

How did you become a member of the Club of Rome, Dr. Weizsäcker?

WEIZSÄCKER: I had the privilege of meeting with Aurelio Peccei at a dinner and lecture in New York in 1983 celebrating the inauguration of the World Resources Institute. One of the persons encouraging me to go there was my Ethiopian friend Professor Aklilu Lemma, a member of the Club of Rome. Ever since then, I have remained in touch with the Club, and in 1991, when I became the founding president of the Wuppertal Institute for Climate, Environment and Energy, the Club's secretary general, Bertrand Schneider, and our mutual friend Martin Lees from the United Kingdom visited me in Bonn and discussed the agenda of the Club. A little later, I received an official invitation to join the Club as a member.

At my first membership meeting, in Buenos Aires, I met with Dr. Alexander King and Dr. Ricardo Díez-Hochleitner and was truly impressed. With Ricardo, I had many fruitful encounters, including in the preparation of the world exposition held in Hanover in 2000 (Expo 2000, Hanover), for which he served as chairman of the international advisory board.

It was through the Club that I learned of you, President Ikeda. Aurelio Peccei mentioned you during that lecture at the Waldorf Astoria Hotel. Later on, of course, Dr. Díez-Hochleitner and others spoke to me about you.

Homo economicus

IKEDA: I still remember the words of Dr. Díez-Hochleitner, who inherited the spirit embodied by Dr. Peccei: "Tomorrow is too late. We must do something today. A sense of crisis drives my work because the problems humanity confronts are too big, too profound, and too urgent."[13] He went on to say that, though his contribution might be insignificant, he must think and act for the sake of humanity.

Acting on one's own initiative, not because one is told to: Both

Dr. Peccei and Dr. Díez-Hochleitner were motivated by a compelling sense of responsibility to the future, by the conviction that they had to do something to make the world a better place. After the publication of *The Limits to Growth*, the Club of Rome was frequently attacked as a group of naysayers or prophets of doom, but I think that the reason the group overcame this barrier of ignorance and exerted such a consciousness-transforming impact on people around the world is this impassioned commitment to stand up and take positive action, as embodied by such people as Dr. Peccei and Dr. Díez-Hochleitner.

As an honorary Club member, I have also delivered regular messages to the world based on my sense of responsibility to the future. Every year on January 26, SGI Day, I continue to offer a new peace proposal in the spirit of working in solidarity with the Club of Rome. You've also embodied the spirit of the Club, resolutely pursued your research, and continued to speak out.

WEIZSÄCKER: Since becoming a member of the Club of Rome, in the course of my work beginning with the Wuppertal Institute,[14] I was invited to prepare a report to the Club three times.

The first was *Factor Four: Doubling Wealth, Halving Resource Use,* published in German in 1995 and later in English and ten other languages, including Japanese and Chinese. It was co-authored by Amory B. Lovins and L. Hunter Lovins, and featured fifty examples of quadrupling resource productivity.

The second, published in 2005, was *Limits to Privatization: How to Avoid Too Much of a Good Thing.* It was co-edited with Oran Young and Matthias Finger, and describes many successful and unsuccessful attempts to seek a fair balance between public responsibility and private-sector efficiency. Some of the inspiration came from Elinor Ostrom, the pioneer of the economics of the commons and 2009 Nobel Prize laureate.

The third report is *Factor Five,* published in English in 2009 and co-authored by Karlson Charlie Hargroves and his Australian team. It goes a lot deeper than *Factor Four* into the politics of the transition we need to see happen. I feel greatly privileged by the repeated invitations I've received to prepare reports to the Club.

Ikeda: It's an outstanding record of achievement.

Though Dr. Peccei and Dr. Díez-Hochleitner are, of course, products of European culture, and my background is, naturally, East Asian civilization, all three of us lived at a time when contemporary science-and-technology-based civilization came to dominate the entire world, and we all reached the decisive conclusion that the transformation of our world must begin with the individual's transformation.

I still remember as if it were yesterday Dr. Peccei coming to our first meeting, in May 1975, carrying a copy of the English translation of my novel *The Human Revolution*. With the exuberance of a youth, he showered me with questions about my philosophy of human revolution. I got a clear sense of his earnest desire to understand. As our dialogue unfolded, he said that our external resources are limited, but our inner wealth unlimited. It is untapped, and human revolution is what allows us to bring it forth. We must make use of every available means to forward that human revolution, he said.[15]

In fact, he had previously used the term "humanistic revolution" himself. After our dialogue, he began to use "human revolution" to indicate the fundamental revolution needed in human existence and life. As I mentioned earlier, the subtitle of my dialogue with Dr. Díez-Hochleitner is *Looking to a Human Revolution*; for the Japanese edition, the literal meaning was "human revolution and global transformation."

And now, our dialogue is beginning with the theme of global transformation in humanity and the environment. It's my hope that our dialogue will carry on the spirit of Dr. Peccei and Dr.

Díez-Hochleitner, and be a powerful voice for global transformation starting with human revolution.

WEIZSÄCKER: I also think that the concept of human revolution is very important. It should be the foundation for all types of education.

IKEDA: In *Factor Five*, you offer a perceptive analysis of the human condition, Dr. Weizsäcker. You argue for the need to transform our view of human nature that has prevailed since the seventeenth-century English philosopher Thomas Hobbes—the belief that we are by nature selfish, materialistic, and in fierce competition with one another. Instead, you focus on our inherent cooperative, accommodating nature and our willingness to seek happiness in tandem with others.

The basic model of human nature that has been put forth by our global market economy is of *Homo economicus*—human beings as dominated by the logic of profit and self-interest. It cannot be denied that this tendency does exist in human beings.

The maxim frequently mentioned in connection with Hobbes, "Man to man is an arrant wolf,"[16] can be traced back to ancient Rome, I believe. But in fact, in the introduction to Hobbes's *De Cive* (Philosophical Rudiments Concerning Government and Society), in which this appears, Hobbes juxtaposes it with another ancient Roman maxim, "Man to man is a kind of God."[17] Hobbes says that both are equally true—man preys upon man, like a wolf, but also regards humankind as something sacred. Hobbes himself recognized that we possess both a selfish nature and a nature that values justice and love.

Of course, we cannot deny the fact that the view of human beings as selfish and predatory beings, like wolves, has come to dominate human history. Unfortunately, this view of humanity and the spread of modern capitalism have amplified and exacerbated each other as they developed in tandem.

WEIZSÄCKER: I would not have paid much attention to the anthropological views of an English philosopher from 350 years ago had this concept of humans as selfish beasts not gained dominance over the world. The *Homo economicus* paradigm had been restricted essentially to the Anglo-American cultures until about 1990. But after the victory of the "Free West" over authoritarian communism, this Anglo-American culture, with all its prejudices and preconceptions, assumed the leading role worldwide.

Financial markets concentrated in the United States and London began forcing companies worldwide to remodel themselves to maximize their shareholder value. Hostile takeovers were seen as a perfectly legitimate means of maximizing returns on investments. Even nation-states, once the proud sovereigns over their legal structures, were blackmailed into changing their rules to the advantage of investors.

RUNAWAY CAPITALISM

IKEDA: Neoliberalism and globalization have made life more convenient and brought a great deal of material wealth to a limited group of people, but they have also caused great harm. Robert B. Reich, a professor at the University of California, Berkeley, who has long warned of the dangers of runaway capitalism and served as secretary of labor during the Clinton administration, has observed, "The last several decades have involved a shift of power away from us in our capacities as citizens and toward us as consumers and investors."[18]

This weakening of civil society is clearly apparent in Japan in recent years. There has been a deterioration of interpersonal relationships in neighborhoods and workplaces, and a weakening of community structures. All of this has left people feeling isolated and alienated. The confluence of multiple factors is eating away at society's foundations.

The free market ideology and modern society in general unconditionally affirm human desires and employ them as the trigger for growth. There may be strengths to this approach, but its excessive emphasis on materialism also leads to a failure to foster our higher natures and the ethos needed to build a society based on mutual cooperation and harmonious coexistence. As Buddhism would put it, the ethical foundation for controlling the "three poisons" of greed, anger, and foolishness—the fundamental earthly desires, or the sources of illusions and base impulses inherent in life that give rise to suffering—has been lost, and the competitive structures of the market economy invade every aspect of our lives, creating a society of harsh, dog-eat-dog, economic domination and subjugation.

WEIZSÄCKER: The logic of financial selfishness is seen as some kind of natural law, as inescapable and even morally superior to every alternative. The rhetoric of the Anglo-American creed depicts the alternatives as authoritarian and as anti-progress, and Nazi tyranny, communism, and Islamic fundamentalism are depicted as the only alternatives to unbridled market capitalism in this simplistic worldview.

At the same time, humans worldwide are ravaging nature's treasures, destabilizing the Earth's climate, and destroying biodiversity. Financial markets don't care about the environment as long as its destruction doesn't hurt the bottom line.

If we want a sustainable ecology, Europeans and Asians should perhaps form a new alliance that philosophically overcomes the view of the "selfish beast" and agrees on international rules rewarding sustainable businesses and lifestyles while penalizing or prohibiting destruction. Such an alliance, however, will only work if it is built upon a common advantage over the competing team. Creating this advantage is one of the hidden motives for the book *Factor Five*. If European and Asian countries, most of which depend heavily on imported resource, learn to become five times more efficient in the use of such resources, their economies will thrive and outperform the countries that are slow at adopting this approach and still insist on unrestricted use of all resources.

IKEDA: It's a very interesting proposal. If we are to successfully resolve our environmental problems, we need not only the awareness that we are all neighbors on this planet but also a responsible vision of society in the future.

WEIZSÄCKER: I tend to believe that Hobbes's view of humans is much too narrow indeed. All major religions offer views of humans as potentially generous, insightful, and willing to subject themselves to higher community goals and to divinity. I do agree, however, with the views of Hobbes and Adam Smith that humans typically orient themselves to what benefits them and their kin.

Hence, I believe that government should modify the framing conditions for economic activity in such a way that this instinctively selfish behavior more or less conforms to the long-term benefits not only of individuals but of all humanity and indeed all life on Earth. This is the anthropological justification for my proposal of a steady increase in energy prices.

IKEDA: In one of his most important treatises, Nichiren wrote, "If you care anything about your personal security, you should first of all pray for order and tranquillity throughout the four quarters of the land, should you not?"[19] If we seek lasting security and prosperity for ourselves and our countries, we need to think and act based on consideration for the peace and prosperity of other countries and the world as a whole. This reflects the awareness that no country can be truly safe when any other country is in danger. We all need to subscribe to a value system in which we and our countries exist in shared security and mutual prosperity.

Buddhism teaches the way of the bodhisattva, who, instead of seeking enlightenment for himself alone, forgoes it until he can awaken all other beings. The bodhisattva's practice is to seek the happiness of both self and others while building a better society. This altruistic way of life is the practical philosophy that we of the SGI strive to embody in our daily lives.

In order to transform the status quo today—the world's unchecked consumption and struggle over limited resources driven by an apparently insatiable desire for more of everything— we need a revolution of the human spirit, what we call *human revolution*, not only on the individual level but also in the underlying ethos of global society. Fresh ideas and policies based on middle- and long-term visions are needed.

We of the SGI want to join forces with the Club of Rome and you to help create a better future for us all.

A World Without War

IKEDA: Of all my meetings with world leaders, one in particular stands out—my meeting and dialogue with your uncle, Richard von Weizsäcker, the first president of the reunited Germany. He invited me to the president's residence in Bonn in June 1991. I still vividly recall our discussions on various topics—efforts for peace in the post-Cold War world, the role of the United Nations, and numerous other subjects—at a critical point immediately following German unification.

President Weizsäcker was praised as the "conscience of Germany" and as a great thinker and statesman. He reflected on your family's tradition in his memoir, *From Weimar to the Wall: My Life in German Politics*, published in 1999, of actively participating, through the generations, in the major issues of their times. Their personal experiences, again and again, were deeply intertwined with historical developments. This is a perceptive assessment of your family's tradition, as President Weizsäcker said, to rise to the challenges of the age and contribute positively to society's development across a broad spectrum of fields.

Your father, Carl Friedrich von Weizsäcker, was an eminent

nuclear physicist and philosopher with a keen understanding of his times and the human condition. I understand that he was also engaged in efforts for peace and was a widely respected public figure, being nominated as a presidential candidate.

It is clear to me that you have succeeded your father's spirit of public service and concern for our planet. As a leading thinker in environmental policy, you have acted consistently from a global perspective, serving as the director at the UN Centre for Science and Technology for Development and being elected to the German parliament. Your life has indeed been a succession of bold challenges, tackling the manifold issues of our day.

WEIZSÄCKER: During my childhood, I was not aware of any such thing as a family tradition. In a sense, it was not until I read Martin Wein's book *Die Weizsäckers* that I learned about some of my ancestors. Of course, I had heard about my great grandfather, Karl Hugo von Weizsäcker, who served as Württemberg's prime minister before World War I, and that others among my ancestors had reached the intellectual heights of their times. I also knew of the extremely difficult and painful time my grandfather, Ernst Heinrich von Weizsäcker, spent at the Foreign Office during the Nazi period. He did not entirely avoid guilt and was sentenced during the Nuremberg Trials to seven years in prison—later reduced to five years upon the intervention of international supporters, including Sir Winston Churchill.

I am proud that at present our family is following its tradition of engagement with the political dimensions of the sciences and in politics itself.

WARTIME MEMORIES

IKEDA: I learned from Wein's book how your grandfather, Ernst Heinrich von Weizsäcker, attempted to restrain the immoral, inhumane foreign policies of the Nazis under Hitler's leadership, and the tremendous distress this caused him. Wein includes in his book something your grandfather said the year before he died:

> In opposing the war, I tried to follow the way of sober objectivity. This was a failure. The proof is in the pudding. What I should have done is attempt the impossible. . . . Only those who sacrifice everything achieve enduring results and still remain true to their convictions.[1]

Your grandfather's anguished words made a deep impression on me. As we discuss your life and your family history, I hope we can highlight the lessons that twentieth-century history has to teach us, as reflected in your grandfather's words.

Let me start by telling you a bit about my own history. I was born in Tokyo in January 1928. As you know, the following year, the great stock market crash brought down Wall Street, and ensuing global panic led to the Great Depression, which had a tremendous effect on nations around the world. It caused social unrest in Japan, and then, in 1931, the Manchurian Incident[2] took place. In 1933, Japan withdrew from the League of Nations, and from that moment on, until it was defeated in World War II, Japan followed the road of militarism.

My childhood was spent in a society under this dark cloud of militarism, and our family home was destroyed in the war. In addition, I contracted tuberculosis, and my own situation, as well as what was taking place in Japanese society, inevitably compelled me as a youth to think a great deal about life and death.

What was your youth like, Dr. Weizsäcker?

WEIZSÄCKER: I was born in June 1939, so I have only a few memories of World War II. Most of what I know of that time is through other people's stories. One thing I do remember, however, is being told that when I was four years old—we lived in Württemberg back then—I announced, "I am now going to the air-raid shelter." My family members said, "But there is no air-raid alert!" Apparently I insisted, "I can hear American airplanes," and went down into the basement. Ten minutes later, the alert sounded. I evidently had very good hearing and could hear faint, distant sounds very well—apparently better than professional air alert folk. But, of course, this is an anecdote that was told to me; personally, I cannot remember it at all.

What I do know is that, through family relationships on my mother's side, we went to Switzerland sometime in 1944. My father somehow smuggled us in, and there we were. And in May 1945, our nanny came storming through the house saying, "The war is over!" I remember which room I was in at the time—the bathroom, as a matter of fact.

IKEDA: I will never forget the day the war ended for Japan, August 15, 1945. I was seventeen, and I heard the announcement that the war was over on the radio, in the home of relatives with whom we were staying in Magome in Omori, Tokyo, having had to evacuate from our own home. I listened with great concentration to what was being said, but the static was so loud that it was hard to make out the words. My younger brother, who must have heard the news somewhere else, came home crying, "Japan lost, Japan lost." I remember feeling tremendously relieved that we wouldn't have to worry about the sound of approaching bombers and realizing how quiet everything was. The blackout regulations were rescinded, and we could turn on the lights in the house at night. I remember my mother rejoicing like a little girl as she prepared our evening meal, saying: "How bright it is! The lights are on. How bright!"

My father recited the names of each of my brothers away fighting. "They'll all come back now," he said, shedding tears of joy. "One from Burma and three from China. They'll all come home."

But though the demobilization process began, my older brothers didn't come home for some time. The three who were in China finally returned the year after the war ended in a completely debilitated condition, but we had no news of the whereabouts of my eldest brother in Burma (present-day Myanmar), and we waited anxiously day after day. Finally, in May 1947, two years after the end of the war, we received a report that he had died in Burma on January 11, 1945. I can still see the image of my mother, her back turned to me and her shoulders trembling as she wept, clutching the telegram in her hand.

When did your family return to Germany after the war?

WEIZSÄCKER: We were allowed to stay in Switzerland until 1948 and were able to rent an apartment in Göttingen, Germany, for the entire family. The University of Göttingen, not destroyed by the war, was the first university to open after the war and became the temporary home of the Max Planck Society,[3] to which my father's institute of physics belonged. Five Nobel Prize winners[4] lived in the small town of Göttingen at the time, establishing and epitomizing an atmosphere of the highest intellectual aspiration and of peacefully overcoming the evil mentality exemplified by Hitler's tyranny. I believe that this atmosphere, which also prevailed in our family, greatly shaped my beliefs.

My uncle, Richard Karl von Weizsäcker, too, was living in Göttingen at the time as a student of law at the university; actually, he lived with us in our flat. He had survived the war and was highly motivated to establish a peaceful trajectory for our country. Of course, we were very much aware of the Soviet Union's dominance over Eastern Europe and its clearly professed intent to subject the world to communist rule, which we considered a permanent threat to peace and to our freedom. Göttingen was a mere fifteen kilometers from the Iron Curtain.[5]

In the peaceful postwar era in West Germany, protected by

American and British troops against the nightmare of communist expansion, I acquainted myself with the virtues of freedom, democracy, and peace.

THE GÖTTINGEN MANIFESTO

IKEDA: Your description presents a clear account of Göttingen's noble tradition as a center of scholarship enduring through wartime trials. War robs young people of their opportunities to study. We of the wartime generation in Japan had that bitter experience.

I was motivated to begin practicing Buddhism, pursue a philosophy of the dignity of life, and get involved in concerted activities for peace by my encounter with Josei Toda, who later became the second president of the Soka Gakkai. I'll never forget our first meeting. It took place on August 14, 1947, a day before the second anniversary of the war's end. I was powerfully impressed by his imposing character as he warmly embraced and encouraged me, a nineteen-year-old whom he was meeting for the first time.

Mr. Toda, along with the founder and first president of the Soka Gakkai, Makiguchi, was imprisoned for his opposition to the policies of Japan's military government during the war; he was a true champion for peace, surviving two years of incarceration during the war. Knowing this, I was certain that he was a person in whom I could place my full trust, and I decided to dedicate my life to following and supporting him as my mentor. It is no exaggeration to say that my youth during the war and my encounter with Mr. Toda when I was seeking the path to peace were the two decisive factors shaping my life.

Taking President Makiguchi's and President Toda's struggle for peace and human rights as our starting point, the SGI has kept their spiritual legacy alive, engaging in a grassroots movement of dialogue and consciousness-raising in numerous countries around the world, aiming to create a sustainable global society and a world without war or nuclear weapons.

Your father's determined efforts to eliminate nuclear weapons are famous, of course.

WEIZSÄCKER: In April 1957, my father took the initiative with seventeen other physicists—the so-called Göttingen 18—to communicate to Federal Chancellor Konrad Adenauer and Minister of Defense Franz Josef Strauss that, above all, they as physicists refused to be part of a program of nuclear armament for Germany, issuing the Göttingen Manifesto. They were outraged by Adenauer's statement that nuclear weapons were an extension of traditional artillery, and they declared as physicists that nuclear arms were in a completely different class from conventional weapons, calling any comparison scandalous.

My father—he was comparatively unknown then—had initiated this protest and prompted Otto Hahn,[6] Werner Heisenberg,[7] and other celebrities of the day to sign the Göttingen Manifesto. This provoked a storm of protest from Adenauer and Strauss—Strauss, especially, was furious!

For weeks, this controversy was the subject of dinner conversations among the public. I was eighteen at the time and thus old enough to follow political events. Suddenly, my father made the cover of the popular magazine *Der Spiegel*, and I remember my classmates approaching me to ask what it was all about.

This controversy stirred enormous discussion, naturally also at my home. And through it all, I observed how calmly my father reacted. Although it was an extremely serious matter, he responded in a comparatively calm and levelheaded fashion. He even joked how foolishly Minister of Defense Strauss was acting and then compared him to Federal Chancellor Adenauer, whom he said was responding much more rationally but still found the controversy to be a great source of political irritation.

I learned a great deal through conversations like these and the nuances that my family members explored in such dialogues. My father never made these discussions seem like a school class; he never explained what was happening like a history lesson. Still, it was a remarkable education for me.

IKEDA: Your father's actions, firmly rooted in his deeply held personal convictions, were themselves an important education for you. The year 1957 was a time of heightened world tensions, following such events as the Suez Crisis[8] and the Hungarian Uprising[9] the previous year. When seen against this background, your father's efforts against nuclear armament were extremely courageous.

The Göttingen Manifesto outlines the social duty of scientists as follows:

> Our activity in pure science and its applications, which brings us into contact with many young people in this field, has bestowed upon us a responsibility for the possible consequences of this activity. This is why we cannot keep silent in these political matters.[10]

It also says, "None of the undersigned would be ready in any way to take part in the production, the tests, or the application of atomic weapons."[11]

This manifesto, for which your father was a motivating force, and the Russell-Einstein Manifesto of 1955[12] stand as shining achievements of scientists of sound moral conscience during the Cold War. I published the dialogue *A Quest for Global Peace* with Dr. Joseph Rotblat, who was at the time of our dialogue the last surviving signatory of the Russell-Einstein Manifesto and who continued to take the lead in the struggle to ban nuclear weapons as secretary-general of the Pugwash Conferences on Science and World Affairs.

As I'm sure you know, 1957 was not only the year of the Göttingen Manifesto but also the first meeting of the Pugwash Conferences in Canada. Coincidentally, it was also the year that my mentor issued his declaration against nuclear weapons before a meeting of fifty thousand young people,[13] calling nuclear weapons an absolute evil that threatened the very survival of the human race. President Toda, at the conclusion of his declaration, entrusted its implementation to us, his youthful followers. From that time, the Soka Gakkai has been working tirelessly for peace, based on Mr. Toda's declaration.

Referring to this, Dr. Rotblat said:

> We were of like mind, and I regret that I was unable to meet Mr. Toda before he died. I believe that Soka Gakkai International (SGI), beginning with Josei Toda and continuing with you, Dr. Ikeda, and all the dedicated SGI members, [has] shared with the Pugwash Conferences the same goal of creating a world without war and nuclear weapons.[14]

Dr. Rotblat told me that the first Pugwash Conference was originally conceived as a one-time event, but it was so successful that a committee was established to consider making it an ongoing institution. Your father attended the initial committee meeting, which was held in London. Dr. Rotblat told me that the focus of the Pugwash Conference activities was discussed at this meeting. Your father clearly played an important role on numerous historic occasions of this sort.

In his efforts to ban nuclear armaments, did he ever speak to you about Japan, the only country against which nuclear weapons have been used?

A Terrible Reality

WEIZSÄCKER: My father visited Japan a couple times, but I believe he never went to Hiroshima and Nagasaki. He did, however, have many Japanese friends for whom the atomic weapons dropped on Hiroshima and Nagasaki were a terrible reality.

Naturally, we spoke of those events. Incidentally, it is interesting that Georg Picht, of whom I spoke before and who was a very close friend of my father, wrote a book around 1980 titled *Hier und Jetzt: Philosophieren nach Auschwitz und Hiroshima* (Here and Now: Philosophizing after Auschwitz and Hiroshima). In it, he suggested that while the fall of Germany was indeed the fault of Germany, the fall of Japan was the fault of the United States, directly because of its bombing of Hiroshima and Nagasaki. In any case, at the time in Germany, we often talked about Hiroshima and Nagasaki, including with our schoolteachers.

My father also told me about being interned in England immediately after Germany's defeat in World War II. Back then, the English had captured some leading physicists and deported them to a secret location in England. This was done to prevent the Russians from capturing the physicists. It had to be executed in secret, or the KGB could have kidnapped them without delay, even in England. As a result, for six months, my mother didn't know the whereabouts of my father. He just disappeared! All she had was the intuitive feeling that he was with the right people.

IKEDA: Clearly, your parents had a relationship built on absolute mutual trust.

Professor Picht, as we discussed earlier, was not only a close friend of your father but remained true to his belief in peace. In the work you mentioned, *Hier und Jetzt: Philosophieren nach Auschwitz und Hiroshima*, Picht wrote, "I learned from Carl Friedrich von Weizsäcker in February 1939 that I had also witnessed the beginning of the nuclear age."[15] In other words, your father visited Picht after Otto Hahn had succeeded in discovering uranium fission (in December 1938), at a point when the means for building an atomic weapon were coming to be understood.

In *Wohin gehen wir?* (Where Are We Going?), his compiled lectures at the University of Munich in early 1997, your father recalls that conversation with Picht. The two men came to three conclusions:

First, if the way to build nuclear weapons were discovered, someone somewhere on the planet would set about producing them.

Second, if a nuclear weapon were successfully produced, given the present state of humanity, someone would make use of it in war.

And third, nuclear weapons are a warning to our age of science and technology. As long as the act of warfare continues to exist as an accepted policy of nation states, scientific technology will be directed to the development of new weapons, and they will be used.[16]

To the world's great misfortune, these very prescient observations have all come true.

WEIZSÄCKER: My father learned of the atomic bomb dropped on Hiroshima while he was interned in England. We had no news or communications from him at the time, but later he told us how the group had heard of the incident in Hiroshima—they were allowed to listen to the radio—and how Otto Hahn had been present and suddenly reproached himself horribly, "What have I done by discovering the fission of uranium!"

That was of course a pivotal statement of enormous import, as was his later declaration, "We do not wish to support nuclear weapons, by no means support them, and we do not wish to permit them!" After that, heavily influenced by the Hiroshima experience, he became deeply involved in the Nuclear Non-Proliferation Treaty and other similar activities.

IKEDA: With the lengthy Cold War tensions that followed, the nuclear arms race, unfortunately, accelerated and expanded.

In August 1961, a wall rose dividing Berlin into eastern and western sectors.

THE BERLIN WALL COMES DOWN

WEIZSÄCKER: We lived in Hamburg at the time, but it was August, so we were in Austria on vacation, staying at a very simple place surrounded by mountain pastures. There was no electricity, no radio, except that my father had a small transistor radio, and eventually the news reached us up there. That's really all I knew about it. Of course we read about it in the newspaper, and it was a shock, but it did not affect us immediately.

IKEDA: Actually, I visited West Berlin just two months after the start of the Wall's construction. There were traces of machine gun fire on Bernauer Street, perhaps from shots fired at people trying to flee East Berlin. I stood in front of Brandenburg Gate. Rising there ominously and separating people from their loved ones, the Wall was a symbol of the devilish nature of power and authority.

I was firmly convinced, even then, that the day would come when the power of the people would bring the Wall down. I also remember making a firm pledge that we young people had to initiate a movement for dialogue to overcome the mistrust and antagonism that enabled such a wall to exist. Because of this, I was incredibly moved when, twenty-eight years later, in 1989, the Wall was torn down, and Germany was reborn as a united country.

As I said earlier, my meeting with President Richard von Weizsäcker a year and a half after the fall of the Wall, eight months after Germany was reunited, is an indelible memory. In 1981, when he became mayor of West Berlin, he said that the Wall was an anti-human construction, the manifestation in stone of a government that denied our innate humanity, and as such its destruction would be a triumph of humanity.[17]

WEIZSÄCKER: It's no wonder that my uncle, Richard von Weizsäcker, saw the Iron Curtain and later the Berlin Wall as symbols of backward and inhuman ideology.

When the Wall came down in 1989, I was fifty years old and lived in Bonn, then Germany's capital, directing the Institute for European Environmental Policy. Had anybody asked me half a year before the event if I was praying for German reunification, I would have said it was so far removed from any realistic possibility that I would not even consider it. And yet, when it happened, we all felt enormous relief. As did everyone in Europe, I celebrated it wholeheartedly.

To us in Germany, it was clear that it had been Willy Brandt's détente policy[18] in the early 1970s that had allowed the emergence of conditions that eventually led to the peaceful "Gorbachev transition." Mikhail Gorbachev, then president of the Soviet Union, seemingly prevented the hawks in his country and in East Germany (German Democratic Republic) from intervening in the peaceful transition. We had no sympathy for the view from America that it was President Ronald Reagan's uncompromising confrontation with the "evil empire" that brought communism down.

IKEDA: It's unfortunate that the end of the Cold War has been simplistically interpreted in some quarters as the unalloyed victory of the West and the triumph of capitalism, reinforcing the shift to the neoliberalism and unregulated capitalism. And now, supplanting ideological differences, the new focus of conflict being touted is this so-called Clash of Civilizations,[19] which has exacerbated tensions in a different form and kept the sword of Damocles of nuclear armaments—the toxic legacy of the Cold War—hanging over our heads two decades after the Cold War's end.

It may well be true that the threat of nuclear Armageddon and the resulting extinction of the human race have diminished since the Cold War ended. But the proliferation of nuclear weapons continues unabated, and the danger that they will be employed in escalating regional conflicts continues to grow.

In *Der ungesicherte friede* (The Insecure Peace), your father warned, "The possession of such weapons as a deterrence in hope of never having to deploy them is a gallop over Lake Constance, a dance over the abyss."[20] Conflict among nations that possess nuclear armaments becomes ever more dangerous as the number of nuclear nations grows.

The SGI has been working with numerous organizations to put a Nuclear Weapons Convention in place that will make the possession of nuclear weapons by any state, without exception, illegal. Currently, cooperating with the International Campaign to Abolish Nuclear Weapons sponsored by the International Physicians for the Prevention of Nuclear War, we're engaged in expanding a network of support for the establishment of such a convention. In 2010, Soka Gakkai youth in Japan delivered a petition with 2.27 million signatures to the United Nations secretary-general and the chairman of the Review Conference of the Parties to the Treaty on the Non-Proliferation of Nuclear Weapons.

In addition, in conjunction with numerous other organizations, we're sponsoring the exhibition *From a Culture of Violence to a Culture of Peace* in various locales around the world. In October 2011, we presented the exhibition with the Global Cooperation Council and the IPPNW Germany as cosponsors in Berlin. Despite your busy schedule, you presented an address on this occasion, "Peacemaking: A European-Asian Alliance." Thank you so much. I've heard that your presentation was well received.

WEIZSÄCKER: Thank you. The various exhibitions held by the SGI are very important because of the role they play in raising awareness on the individual level of the importance of abolishing nuclear weapons. This is critical in building a majority committed to creating peace, embracing individuals representing the broadest possible spectrum of religious, philosophical, and political beliefs.

Curiosity Set Free

IKEDA: I am grateful for your warm understanding. To return to your father, his achievements, ideas, and actions are quite well known in Japan through his numerous writings translated into Japanese. You contributed the foreword to the Japanese edition of your father's book *Wohin gehen wir?* In it, you described him as a "contemporary who has continued to speak out passionately to the present day about the possibility of how the human race can eliminate the institution of war and its accompanying structures," and said that "he has identified the difficulty of understanding human behavior when we restrict our viewpoint to the actions of the individual, and stressed the essential importance of interpreting human actions in their larger context."[21] Clearly, you have a profound understanding of your father.

WEIZSÄCKER: Only much later did I learn that my father was one of the greatest physicists and philosophers of his time. I was already an adult when he became really active in nuclear disarmament and in peace research, and I was absolutely convinced he was right in doing so and felt that all scientists should do the same.

He was a wonderful person and father. He loved to joke and was particularly good at playing with language. He was kind and possessed great intellectual curiosity.

He appreciated my rather erratic and childish nature as a boy. He tolerated my "maverick" or unruly habits and openly supported my curiosity about exciting biological phenomena, such as the transformation of caterpillars into chrysalis and later butterflies.

IKEDA: You've given me a clear impression of your father as a man with powerful curiosity, an open mind, an active interest in everything going on in the world around him, and the desire to understand it—the impression that your father clearly made on you as well. Your siblings have followed in your father's footsteps, becoming scholars in economics, theology, and mathematics. In addition, your mother was a historian.

WEIZSÄCKER: My mother was from a large Swiss family (the Wille family), and she was a very generous person who supported her husband and her children to the best of her capacity. She was generally more concerned with keeping the house in order and making her children follow established rules than my father was, and she had a very independent mind in political matters.

She enjoyed company, and we had guests and friends filling our home, first in Göttingen, later in Hamburg. When I acted up as a child, she was considerably more critical of my behavior than my father, but in the end, she was also fairly tolerant as well. In my family, I had the privilege of participating in scientific, political, and philosophical discussions as a boy, and later, I was allowed to pursue my own scientific interests in biology and physics.

IKEDA: It's wonderful that in your family, the children were allowed to take part in adult discussions, instead of being excluded because the topics were regarded as "too difficult" for children's ears. You used the word *participate*. Participation is very important, I believe. For children, the experience of being acknowledged as a person and granted a legitimate place in the family and society is an important step in the process of becoming an adult.

What motivated you to select biology and physics as your subjects of study? Was there some early childhood experience that led you to this choice?

WEIZSÄCKER: The beauty of nature, a fascination with living creatures, with butterflies, caterpillars, fish, birds. I was more attracted to animals than flowers and plants—particularly the kinds of animals that are not always the typical favorites of children, such as polliwogs, newts, caterpillars, butterflies, and beetles.

IKEDA: You displayed the same strong curiosity as a boy that your father had.

As far as my own education goes, I received instruction not only in Buddhist philosophy but also a broad variety of subjects from my mentor. As well as having unwavering faith in the principles and perspectives of Buddhism, Mr. Toda prized the pursuit of universal knowledge and wisdom. He often stressed the importance of contact with great individuals—even if it only meant listening to what they had to say from a distance, in a large auditorium. This, he said, is the best way to learn and is always worthwhile.

Many eminent individuals have visited Soka University of Japan and spoken to the students there—Mikhail Gorbachev, former Chilean president Patricio Aylwin Azócar, environmental activist Wangari Maathai, and numerous others. In 2000, we were honored to have you speak there. These occasions are a source of tremendous inspiration for our students. Soka University representatives tell me that they would like to have you speak at the university again.

I'm sure you have had many encounters in your youth with individuals who inspired you both personally and intellectually.

WEIZSÄCKER: Partly through my father, I met some of the true geniuses of the time. Among them were Werner Heisenberg, the physicist and nuclear scientist Leo Szilard, the biophysicist Max Delbrück, the zoologist and ethnologist Konrad Lorenz, and the behavioral physiologist Erich von Holst.

IKEDA: This is certainly an impressive roster of scientists! I once spoke to Soka University students about Werner Heisenberg, who made fundamental contributions to quantum theory. I told them how, when he was ordered by the Nazis to join the team working on uranium fission, he remained faithful to his principles by telling the Nazis that the development of nuclear weapons was fraught with difficulties, thus slowing their development.

If you recall any particular statements or episodes from your encounters with these great scientists, I hope you will share them with our readers, especially youth.

WEIZSÄCKER: My most important encounter was with Professor Leo Szilard, a colleague and friend of Einstein. He came to visit our home about six months before I was to graduate from the gymnasium (secondary school) and asked me, "What do you want to be?"

I replied, "'I want to become a biologist."

"Yes, that is very interesting, but then, of course, you must not study biology."

I didn't understand what he meant. And then he said: "Well, what they teach in biology today is outdated. First, study physics or chemistry or math or even medicine and learn something sensible. Later on, you can apply that knowledge to biology."

Back then, this was a very surprising statement. Yet, I essentially complied with it and studied chemistry and, later, physics. I only took up biology during my doctoral studies. So, in this case, an interesting guest visiting our home had a major impact on my life.

OF PRACTICAL USE

IKEDA: I think a distinguishing feature of your scholarly work is that you always find a way to put your research to effective use in society. What prompted you to adopt this pattern of applying your scholarly results in the real world?

WEIZSÄCKER: I do not remember a specific incident, but I believe the wish to be of practical use is the most natural thing in the world. Actually, everybody wants that.

Today's academia is constrained by the fact that practical utility is equated with economic utility. We must rebel against this trend, as this means that all learning is appropriated for immediate gain and private profit, and all long-term durability—academic freedom, in a sense—is destroyed.

If the opportunity arises to make a positive contribution, everybody, in practice, does so. Professor Georg Picht was the head of the Protestant Institute for Interdisciplinary Research (Forschungsstätte der Evangelischen Studiengemeinschaft, or FEST) in Heidelberg, where I had my first position after receiving my doctorate. He told us young beginners, "You must always work on a topic that is scientifically rigorous, represents fresh territory, but in parallel, you should also do work that is of practical relevance. . . ."

My first practical study was on disarmament issues regarding biological weapons. I established a task force for open systems and one for biological weapons. Picht was very pleased. He praised our group for coming up with new topics, both of which had practical, concrete applications. My three years at the institute taught me the importance of combining theory and practice.

When the problem of biological and chemical weapons was halfway resolved and the negotiations in Geneva had nearly ended, I shifted to human ecology as my new subject of study at FEST. I began these studies in 1971. The first head of environment at Germany's Department of the Interior was on our task force, and we wrote a book on human ecology and environmental protection. It seems to have helped in the formulation of environmental policy in Bonn.

IKEDA: This was your real start with environmental issues, then.

When the Biological Weapons Convention[22] went into effect in

1975, your first subject of research, biological weapons disarmament, was on the path toward a satisfactory resolution. Subsequently, the Chemical Weapons Convention went into effect in 1997. Today, most nations regard the use of biological or chemical weapons as deplorable, and there is a growing consensus in global society that even their possession is a disgrace.

As I said earlier, with the proliferation of nuclear weapons and the rising danger that they will be accidentally employed, there is an urgent need to establish an international legal framework, following in the footsteps taken to ban biological and chemical weapons, that outlaws all nuclear armaments, the most inhumane of all weapons. In response to the peace proposal I issued in 2011 calling for the prompt adoption of a Nuclear Weapons Convention, Jayantha Dhanapala, who worked on disarmament issues for many years at the United Nations and is now president of the Pugwash Conferences, commented:

> I think we have to acknowledge that issues of life and death transcend global politics and national loyalties. There comes a time in the affairs of men when we have to recognize [that] we have to rise above petty national politics and do things that are for the benefit of humankind and the inheritance of humankind. . . . [W]e have to recognize that the way out is to abolish weapons so that all countries participate in that abolition. There cannot be proliferation if there are no weapons.[23]

I find a great resemblance between Dr. Dhanapala's statement and your father's philosophy as articulated in the Göttingen Manifesto and other forums. In one of those forums, your father stressed that the "political state of the world must be changed fundamentally, so that a true peacekeeping order can arise."[24]

The time has come for we who live in the twenty-first century to wholeheartedly dedicate ourselves to building a world without nuclear weapons.

Green Growth

IKEDA: Nichiren wrote, "A wise person, while dwelling in security, anticipates danger; a perverse one, while dwelling amid danger, takes security for granted."[1] It is essential that we adopt this preemptive approach toward environmental issues, taking the necessary steps now to prevent future crises.

In June 2012, the UN Conference on Sustainable Development will convene in Rio de Janeiro, Brazil. Also known as Rio+20, it marks the twentieth anniversary of the Earth Summit held in Rio in 1992. The conference will look for answers to global environmental problems and hunger, focusing on two themes, "a green economy in the context of sustainable development and poverty eradication" and "the institutional framework for sustainable development."

You represented the German government in the original 1992 Earth Summit, and you helped organize the Johannesburg Earth Summit of 2002 in your capacity as a member of the United Nations' advisory committee. SGI representatives participated in both the 1992 and 2002 summits.[2] I held high hopes for the conferences and contributed an environmental proposal of my own to the 2002 meeting. With the increased awareness of the urgency of environmental issues, the upcoming conference is the focus of intense interest.

WEIZSÄCKER: Just how much of the necessary transition will be promoted and decided at the UN Conference on Sustainable Development in Rio this year [2012] is a completely open question. It is to be feared that we will see ourselves confronted with an alliance between those who earn short-term benefits from squandering resources and those who simply cannot imagine that a green economy is possible.

The idea of a green economy has been a splendid initiative by the UN Environment Programme's executive director, Achim Steiner. Essentially, it means that we can eradicate poverty and enjoy considerable additional growth without jeopardizing nature and climate. This would be a fairly radical breach with today's habits and technologies, which so far almost invariably imply a contradiction between ecology and economy.

IKEDA: The UNEP has issued a report for the upcoming Rio+20 conference expressing the opinion that if appropriate government measures are taken, investing 2 percent of the global GDP in green growth will enable the shift toward a low-carbon, resource-efficient economy while boosting economic growth and keeping human activities within ecologically acceptable limits. We must find ways for nations to work together to build a sustainable global society. One of the keys is no doubt international cooperation in the area of energy policy.

It is said that, at present, the consumption of fossil fuels accounts for nearly 60 percent of the carbon dioxide and other greenhouse gasses. In your book *Factor Five*, you propose an approach to making the shift to a low-carbon, resource-efficient, green economy.

WEIZSÄCKER: My own work on a new cycle of technological progress stems chiefly from the observations that the Earth is limited,
and that further expansion, deeper digging, overfishing, and the
excessive burning of fossil fuels will further and eventually fatally
deteriorate its face and human living conditions. I tried to find
partners who had similar motives and were better than me in discovering and formulating technological answers to the ecological
challenges. Such partners were Amory Lovins and Hunter Lovins
in the United States and, fifteen years later, Karlson Charlie Hargroves and his team from Australia. This is the origin of *Factor Four*
and *Factor Five*.

The *Factor Five* story of producing wealth with one fifth of the
energy and materials currently used is an exciting opportunity
for humankind. In the book, providing a reasonable and realistic
approach, we strive to pave the way to overcome the crisis of global
warming by 2050.

No One's Immune

IKEDA: Global warming will not only have a grave impact on
ecological systems around the world but will also cause climactic
disasters and become a source of conflict, exacerbating poverty
and hunger. It is a challenge to human civilization as a whole,
exemplifying all the global threats of the twenty-first century.

UN Secretary-General Ban Ki-moon has said, "In the longer
run, no one—rich or poor—can remain immune from the dangers brought by climate change."[3] As he indicates, no one can be a
disinterested bystander in the face of the global warming threat.
It is a multifaceted and currently unfolding danger that will have
a profound impact on our children's and grandchildren's generations, a threat that could destroy our future.

Developing technologies and increasing energy efficiency to

prevent the production of greenhouse gases—as well as the adoption of renewable energy sources such as wind, water, and solar power and biomass energy—are themes of considerable importance in both *Factor Four* and *Factor Five*. In particular, you describe energy conservation as the most fiscally efficient method for reducing greenhouse gases, as well as the method with the greatest potential for improvement. I strongly agree.

In Japan, the reduction in electricity generated by nuclear power—resulting from the earthquake and tsunami damage to the Fukushima Daiichi nuclear power plant, which led to the shutdown of other plants as well—has made the establishment of a stable energy supply an important issue for the future. In responding to this problem, not only must we seek to conserve energy in our daily lives, but Japanese society as a whole must make greater efforts at energy conservation. People's attitudes toward energy consumption in Japan are beginning to change dramatically.

WEIZSÄCKER: Between the mid 1970s and the late 1980s, Japan was a world leader in energy productivity. Power and fuel prices were highest there. A few energy-intensive industries such as aluminum smelting from bauxite left Japan and resettled elsewhere, but Japanese industry developed the fifth computer generation, the Shinkansen train, digital imaging, and high tech ceramics, all having positive effects on energy efficiency.

Shinkansen trains offer a high-speed alternative to airplanes and automobiles; digital imaging allows video conferencing, reducing mobility needs; and high-tech ceramics have become the core of energy-efficient high-technology devices. The average energy productivity and the economic performance of Japan increased dramatically during those fifteen years—also proving that high energy prices need not hurt economic well-being.

Later, energy efficiency became an official government policy. Japan introduced the Top Runner Program.[4] It volunteered to host the important Third Session of the Conference of the Parties (COP3) of the climate convention in Kyoto, and thousands of public authorities and private companies joined in the Green Purchasing Network. And in the world of materials efficiency, Japan has been a leader in developing the 3R philosophy—reduce, reuse, recycle—as the core of a cyclical economy. I am confident that Japan can easily maintain its leadership in resource productivity.

Regarding renewable energies, Japan is considerably behind other countries. One of the reasons could be the dominant role in Japan of electrical utilities that relied fully on nuclear power and thus had only minimal interest in energy technologies that could compete with nuclear power.

After the Fukushima Daiichi meltdowns and subsequent troubles, I see scope for some change of direction in your country. My recommendation, however, would be to strategically pursue the efficiency avenue combined with a policy of raising energy prices in a manner that avoids compromising the industrial vitality of the country and thus hurting low-income families.

Beyond the Global Casino

IKEDA: I appreciate your encouraging assessment of Japanese energy policies and your advice for the future.

Dr. Hazel Henderson, with whom I engaged in a dialogue that also included discussions of the environment and energy problems,[5] sent her heartfelt condolences following the March 11, 2011, earthquake and tsunami. She cited the advanced technology and expertise of Japan, suggesting that they would play a critical role in rising to the challenge presented by the disaster. She also offered the possibility that the catastrophe would spur us to develop new technologies and find our way toward economic development based not on competition for limited resources but on cooperation.[6] These, she said, are the pressing issues of our times, and overcoming this disaster aligns with the Buddhist teaching of "changing poison into medicine."[7]

Dr. Henderson has told me that she is a friend of you and your wife. In our dialogue, she expressed the highest estimation of your research and scholarship. She also said she was very appreciative of the foreword that you and your wife contributed to her work *The Politics of the Solar Age: Alternatives to Economics.*

WEIZSÄCKER: I don't remember exactly, but I believe I first met Dr. Henderson at a meeting in Moscow in 1989—I think it was on the occasion when I also met Al Gore and Mikhail Gorbachev. She is a great independent thinker, especially concerning economics. She has a far deeper understanding of economics than I do. She was very active at an early stage in the area of ethical funds for institutional investors—for example, working with the insurance company Calvert Group to draw up a manual for the ethical investment of pension funds (the Calvert-Henderson Quality of Life Indicators).[8] That was back in the early 1990s, so it was very early on. Hazel Henderson also popularized the term the "global casino" and has written an article titled "Rules to Tame the Global Casino."[9]

IKEDA: Dr. Henderson is a strong advocate for revamping our current economic system—which, far from bettering society, has increased the gap between rich and poor and led to the pollution of our environment—and making the transformation to sustainable societies. She sees, as we have been discussing, energy conservation as the key to shifting to a low-carbon, recycling society.

I have also long emphasized the need for Japan, which has considerable experience and concrete achievements in this area, to take the initiative to reach out to its neighboring countries and work together with them to establish a model East Asian energy conservation zone.

In *Factor Five,* you describe the possibility of future increases in energy efficiency and productivity.

WEIZSÄCKER: Indeed, the McKinsey Global Institute in 2007 published a cost estimate for different methods of carbon dioxide abatement, showing that efficiency measures typically were much more cost effective than renewable energies. However, the analysis was essentially static, considering only technologies that were commercially available in 2007.

Factor Five and *Factor Four,* on the other hand, speak about existing and future technologies. In *Factor Five,* we establish the analogy between resource productivity and labor productivity. Labor productivity increased roughly twentyfold in the course of the Industrial Revolution, and none of today's high productivity techniques would have been imaginable in the midst of the nineteenth century.

We also show, in chapter 9 of *Factor Five,* that labor productivity increases were always accompanied by wage increases, which in turn spurred further productivity improvements. Learning from this mutual increase between productivity and cost of one production factor, we argue that a gradual increase of energy and resource prices could lead to a nearly unlimited increase of resource productivity.

Part One of the book, drafted by the Australian team of co-authors—Karlson Charlie Hargroves, Michael Smith, Cheryl Desha, and Peter Stasinopoulos—shows that even in the difficult branches of transport, industry, agriculture, and construction, a fivefold increase of resource productivity and of carbon dioxide efficiency is available using proven technologies.

IKEDA: It's a remarkable discovery. What, for example, can Japan do to move in this direction?

WEIZSÄCKER: Since Japan already has many outstanding engineers and leading international companies and a government that works closely with industry, I suspect that Japanese science and technology and the Japanese economy can very quickly realize the targets of twice the productivity and half the energy consumption—in other words, factor four—and move on to factor five, the 80 percent or fivefold increase in resource productivity and energy efficiency.

For example, let's take the case of the new light-emitting diodes as opposed to the old incandescent light bulbs, an area in which Japan is already a leader. That alone represents a dramatic reduction in energy use, since the new diodes consume only one-tenth of the electricity that the incandescent ones use.

Another example is cement production. A switch from Portland cement to cement manufactured from blast furnace slag from iron production and fly ash from coal-fired power plants represents an energy savings of about 70 to 80 percent. There are numerous other examples, but I will not repeat the information provided in *Factor Five*.

I suspect that, politically, Japan could slowly raise the price of energy, providing economic stimulus for energy efficiency. The problem globally is that energy is too cheap, and therefore the efficiency potentials are not exploited.

Japan has somewhat less favorable geographical conditions than, say, Germany or Denmark regarding renewable energy, and therefore, the transition from coal and nuclear power to renewable energies is more challenging. Since that is difficult for Japan, it is all the more important for Japan to maximize energy efficiency.

IKEDA: While Japan has been engaged in developing energy conservation technology for many years, Germany has been a leader in efforts to build a framework for international cooperation to promote the other key approach to energy savings, renewable energy sources. The International Renewable Energy Agency (IRENA), established in January 2009 through the initiative of Germany as well as Spain and Denmark, is now an important international organization with 148 member nations, having become fully operative in April 2011. In my 2002 peace proposal, I suggested adopting a convention for the promotion of renewable energy and called for international efforts to create policies in this area.

Germany has been a pioneer in this field, with its solar energy production capacities in 2010 greater than the 2009 solar energy production capacity of the entire world. In September 2010, Chancellor Angela Merkel attracted worldwide attention when she announced Germany's goal. At the Second Petersberg Climate Dialogue, she declared, "We intend to raise the share of renewable energies in total energy consumption to 60 percent by 2050 and the share in electricity consumption to 80 percent."[10]

What led to this highly ambitious initiative in Germany to make the shift to renewable energy sources?

WEIZSÄCKER: During the 1980s, the pollution-caused dieback of forests and the Chernobyl nuclear accident[11] caused alarm in Germany, leading to a massive political strengthening of the young Green Party and of an ecological wing in the Social Democratic Party (Sozialdemokratische Partei Deutschlands, or SPD). To fend off their taking the parliamentary majority, the conservative government under Chancellor Helmut Kohl took major steps toward embracing ecological issues. His ecological champion in the government was environment minister Dr. Klaus Töpfer, who later became the executive director of UNEP.

In 1991, Töpfer initiated a pioneering step toward renewable energy, the Electricity Feed-in Law (Stromeinspeisungsgesetz), forcing utilities to pay producers of renewable power a compensation equivalent to the average power cost; this was far from cost coverage for photovoltaics (PV, or solar power) but came close to cost coverage for wind power, actually kicking off an early boom in wind power.

A few years later, when the SPD and Greens finally succeeded in achieving a majority, they introduced the Renewable Energy Act (Erneuerbare Energien Gesetz, or EEG). This law made Germany the world champion of renewable energies, including related technologies. It soon was copied by fifty other countries. The law offered cost-covering compensation to producers of electricity from wind, solar, small-scale hydro, and biomass.

The cost for the compensation was shouldered not by taxpayers but by utilities, who then passed the added cost on to all electricity users. Rising electricity costs were soon criticized by industry, consumers, and later by conservative parties who moved to change the law in three steps, in 2004, 2009, and 2011, always reducing the compensation a bit.

The initiator of the law was Dr. Hermann Scheer, member of parliament, who also conceived and promoted the idea of IRENA. Dr. Scheer was a personal friend of mine for decades. Unfortunately, he died prematurely in 2010.

IKEDA: Dr. Scheer is known in Japan for his writings, including *The Solar Economy (Solare Weltwirtschaft*, 2004). He spent nineteen years in his efforts to establish IRENA. In an interview published in Japan, Dr. Scheer said that renewable energy is the key to bolstering energy security, reinforcing energy supplies to developing and semi-developed countries, and contributing in the long term to lowering energy costs and carbon dioxide emissions.[12] Energy policy cannot be approached solely on the national level but needs to be considered from a global perspective that includes its effects on such problems as climate change and poverty.

Regarding the reinforcement of stable energy supplies to developing and semi-developed countries, I am reminded of the words of President Thomas Jefferson: "He who receives an idea from me, receives instruction himself without lessening mine; as he who lights his taper at mine, receives light without darkening me."[13] Up to now, the nations that have been able to secure stable energy supplies have had the advantage, often creating dramatic gaps and cutthroat competition. But if we intend to achieve a sustainable future, it must be accompanied by changes on a global scale. As IRENA aims, it is important to improve the methods and conditions of bringing energy technology and information to developing countries.

Dr. Scheer commented that technology transfer can be carried out based on commercial patents or outside the system of commercial patents. Cooperation is difficult in the former case, but technology transfer can have broader implications. For example, he stated that joint ventures can enable a company to establish itself in new markets. In addition, training workers and increasing human resource capacities up through the university and research-facility level are also effective. Germany has adopted this approach, with positive results, Dr. Scheer said.[14]

I am reminded of the point you made in your book *Earth Politics* that one of the important post-Cold War political issues should be the elimination of the north-south ecology gap. This issue is reflected in the international energy situation. At the same time, ambitious international projects, such as DESERTEC,[15] which promote the establishment of cooperative energy policies embracing large geographical regions, are beginning to get under way.

WEIZSÄCKER: In 2009, the earlier DESERTEC Foundation, together with Munich Re, the world's largest reinsuring company, and twelve industry conglomerates created the DESERTEC industry initiative (Dii) to promote power cooperation between Europe and the Middle East-North Africa (MENA) region, using chiefly solar power from MENA. The idea was originally created by the Club of Rome, which at the time had its headquarters in Hamburg.

My friends Gerhard Knies and Uwe Möller, then secretary general of the Club of Rome, were the initiators, warmly supported by Prince El Hassan bin Talal of Jordan, then president of the Club of Rome.

DESERTEC is meant to provide European, chiefly German, money and technologies for the construction of Concentrated Solar Power stations in the deserts and the connecting grids allowing transport of the power to Europe. The transmission would use High Voltage Direct Current technologies.

IKEDA: DESERTEC aims by 2050 to provide 15 percent of Europe's electricity needs and the majority of the electricity needs of the nations of North Africa from solar power generated in the north Sahara region. This in itself is a large-scale project, but I've heard that if the entire north Sahara region of 34,750 square miles (90,000 square kilometers) were equipped with solar-power generating facilities, it could produce all the power needed by the entire world. Of course, the establishment of the power-delivery grid and other technological problems remain to be solved, but the project represents an attempt to open new possibilities, and I hope that it proceeds successfully.

I've had many friendly interactions with Prince El Hassan bin Talal of Jordan, whom you mention as one of the project's supporters. Prince Hassan stressed the need to discard narrow-minded nationalism, tribalism, and discrimination, and to construct a new world order based on the principles of human rights and humanism,[16] a view with which we of the SGI agree wholeheartedly.

The prince expressed his agreement with my support, outlined in my proposal to the United Nations' Earth Summit in Johannesburg in 2002, for the establishment of the "UN Decade of Education for Sustainable Development," an initiative promoted by the SGI as a nongovernmental organization in consultative status with the United Nations and in concert with other NGOs. In order to protect the quality of life of the current generation as well as the welfare of future generations, the prince said, we must simultaneously pursue environmental protection, economic prosperity, and social justice, giving priority to education as the way to create a sustainable future.[17]

As you know, the 57th United Nations General Assembly adopted a resolution formally designating the ten-year period starting in 2005 as the "UN Decade of Education for Sustainable Development." In support, the SGI sponsored the two exhibitions *Seeds of Hope* and *Seeds of Change* at various venues around the world as a citizens' consciousness-raising effort. The activism of a network of awakened citizens will be increasingly important to resolve the impasse in the environmental challenges we face, involving as they do various economic and other factors.

Reforms from Below

Weizsäcker: In recent years, states have been systematically weakened and had ever-shrinking funds available to invest in the environment and long-term public interests. Chapter 10 in *Factor Five* calls for the reestablishment of a healthy balance between the public and private sectors. Weakening the private sector is not what we want, so we should concentrate on strengthening the public sector. This is a double agenda: global governance to discourage investors from picking locations with the weakest rules and the strengthening of civil society, inducing it to fight for public interests.

Ikeda: In *Factor Five*, you point to NGOs as an important factor in expanding public interests on a global level, helping to strike a balance with the profit-oriented market economy. You argue that NGOs can "name and shame and help boycott private firms as well as states violating or neglecting important principles related to public goods."[18] In fact, while some seven hundred NGOs were registered with the United Nations Economic and Social Council at the 1992 Earth Summit, today that number has risen to about 3,200, and they are playing an accordingly larger role.

In *Factor Five*, you also say that the reinforcement and reform of the United Nations are no longer completely utopian goals, suggesting that other UN-related organizations, such as the UN Environment Programme, should begin trying to exercise the global sanctions that up to now have only been wielded by the World Trade Organization.[19] Putting aside the question of sanctions, I believe that strengthening international organizations that deal with environmental matters is a matter of pressing concern.

It is noteworthy that an April 2011 statement issued by the German government's Advisory Council on Global Change (Wissenschaftlichen Beirat Globale Umweltveränderungen, or WBGU) called for the establishment of a global environmental institution at the 2012 UN Conference on Sustainable Development (Rio+20). I urged the creation of a similar organization in my 2008 peace proposal.

The institutional framework for sustainable development is the main theme of the Rio+20 conference. I earnestly hope that the conference does not end up another fruitless exercise in mutual accusations about who is responsible for the present crisis but instead, through constructive discussions, opens a way to establish cooperation among all nations based on the common goal of humanity's welfare.

In addition to such top-down reforms, such as changes in government policies, what do you think is especially important to promote people's movements that bring about grassroots reforms?

WEIZSÄCKER: Years ago, I was cofounder of a committee against local pollution in Essen. That was the beginning of the 1970s, when I lived in Essen. Essen was a center of pollution in Germany.

Later, my wife and I lived in a suburb of Bonn, where we sometimes observed a day of remembrance on Hiroshima Memorial Day. When I was in politics as a member of parliament, I cultivated contacts with NGOs much more intensely than other MPs did.

I want to see grassroots movements for the environment and peace serving as inspiring examples for young people, proving that commitment to working for good causes can be much more fulfilling than playing computer games.

IKEDA: The future of movements for peace and the environment rests with young people. The SGI, through its youth organizations in every country, is promoting educational, consciousness-raising activities related to environmental protection, such as tree-planting programs and seminars on the Earth Charter,[20] with its focus on building a sustainable future.

Following the earthquake and tsunami of March 11, 2011, we opened forty-two of our community centers in the affected areas as evacuation centers and engaged in other relief and rescue operations. Numerous young people in our organization, even those who had lost their own homes and families in the disaster, worked hard to assist and encourage others.

Through their examples, they have shown that, no matter how deep the darkness or how fraught with pain and difficulty a situation is, when young people stand up and take positive action, they can make the sun of hope and courage rise again. These admirable young people are continuing to rebuild and restore their communities.

It is my sincere hope that today, in the face of the complex global problems we face, young people will stand up, reach out to one another to establish a global network, and make our world a better place for all.

Sufficiency and Human Fulfillment

IKEDA: What makes a society affluent in the truest sense? What constitutes a truly happy way of life? In order to find fundamental solutions to the environmental challenges we face, we need to reexamine both the presuppositions upon which our societies operate and our own lifestyles.

In the last, eleventh, chapter of *Factor Five,* you focus on precisely those issues. You look deeper than such "hard" aspects as increasing energy efficiency through technological innovation and reducing consumption through revised tax policies and consider the issue from the "soft" aspect of the inner transformation we need to make as individuals.

It is clear that the underlying cause of the environmental destruction that is proliferating on a global scale is an unchecked increase in human desires—in other words, greed. It seems to me that this is the fundamental cause that has given birth to the mass consumer society that the economically advanced nations have enjoyed up to now. But is a society, a civilization, that seems to be engaged in a competition of ever-expanding greed for limited resources and energy truly an affluent society?

In *Factor Five,* you cite an interesting analysis by Richard Hein-berg of data from the United Nations and other sources: The self-reported happiness in Mexico and Venezuela is 20 percent higher than that of the United States, though the people of Mexico and Venezuela use only 25 to 35 percent of the energy per capita com-pared to the United States.[1] Affluence alone does not necessarily correlate to happiness—or, to use your keyword, "sufficiency," in the sense of satisfaction and fulfillment in life.

WEIZSÄCKER: As you kindly point out, sufficiency is the opposite of greed and will be an indispensable feature of all mature civiliza-tions. It will be necessary to persuade masses of people that hap-piness can be attained without wasteful ways of life. One example we cite concerns nutritional habits. More calories consumed in the affluent countries tend to lead not to a more enjoyable life but to obesity.

In *Factor Five,* I wrote:

> Once a certain degree of wealth is reached and is distrib-uted with a degree of fairness, politicians and the broader public need not be afraid if growth and consumption are flattening out, provided other factors supporting happi-ness are strong.[2]

The "other factors" I mention include such happy and rewarding experiences as social solidarity, playing music in groups, enjoy-ing one's children, participating in theater, and so forth. Being permanently in competition for ever more consumption makes it impossible for us to enjoy such experiences. That is why we say in *Factor Five* that a model of humanity like that put forth by Thomas Hobbes, which sees humans as selfish beasts, is not sustainable.

"Sufficiency communities"—communities that value satisfac-tion rather than unlimited consumption—do exist, and they see themselves as rather more advanced, not backward.

IKEDA: In Japan as well, more and more people are seeking to attain spiritual fulfillment through volunteering and strengthening community interaction. You've visited Japan on numerous occasions. How would you say Japanese society has changed in recent years?

The Gift of Biodiversity

WEIZSÄCKER: In the early 1980s, Japan was extremely optimistic and was about to overtake the United States in many areas. Japan had much higher growth rates than the United States, which was facing a serious crisis, a spiritual crisis, in the aftermath of the Vietnam War and the ensuing economic stagflation—the combination of stagnant economic growth and inflation.

That was when the Trilateral Commission of Europe, the United States, and Japan was established. Japan was seen—and saw itself—as on equal footing with Europe and the United States. This mentality, which some people regarded as arrogant—I did not—is now completely absent in Japan.

At the end of the 1980s, Japan's real estate bubble imploded, creating a major economic crisis. This was followed by ten years of economic stagnation, and all attempts to reinvigorate the economy through low interest rates were unsuccessful.

Yet Japan remains an extremely important and prominent nation. It hosted the conference that resulted in the Kyoto Protocol and in Nagoya in 2010 hosted the tenth meeting of the Conference of the Parties to the Convention on Biological Diversity, leading to an anti-biopiracy protocol. Japan has provided several heads of major UN agencies, such as UNESCO, and is the location of the United Nations University.

Japan continues to play a huge role on the international stage, although it seems to me that its earlier enthusiastic optimism has disappeared. But that can come back again.

IKEDA: Japan was still dealing with an extended period of economic stagnation. Then, in 2011, there was the terrible earthquake and tsunami in northeastern Japan. The country is facing a critical moment in its history.

This makes it crucial, I strongly believe, for Japan to look clearly into the future ten and twenty years hence and find a practical, sound pathway to recovery rather than return to the optimism of the past, which proved in many ways to be blind and unfounded.

You mentioned the conference in Nagoya on the Convention on Biological Diversity (the COP10 conference, or tenth Conference of the Parties to the Convention), and you've stressed in various forms the necessity of preserving biological diversity, devoting a whole chapter of your book *Earth Politics* to it. The conclusion is this statement from your wife, Christine von Weizsäcker, which made a deep impression on me:

> Finally, and this is a question of our cultural self-understanding, we should recognize that biodiversity is not just a commodity like oil. It is a unique gift to humanity and it should be seen as a value [in] its own right.[3]

Your wife has long been known as one of the leading activists regarding the issue of biodiversity. She visited Japan to represent the environmental NGO Ecoropa at the Nagoya conference, where she spoke on the importance of ecosystems, pointing out that genetic modification of living organisms is a threat to biodiversity. When did the two of you first become active in this field?

WEIZSÄCKER: Soon after we were married, I established the working group on human ecology at the Protestant research institute FEST Heidelberg, with which my wife later also sometimes participated. Following that, I was at the University of Essen, where

I established a curriculum on the environment. By that time, we already had three children. While I was becoming the founding president of Kassel University and was engaged in my academic career, my wife was busy with four children by then, and it became hard for our family to do everything together.

Christine's intense commitment to the issues of biodiversity and biosafety only became possible when our children were mostly grown, from the early or mid 1990s. After the Earth Summit in Rio de Janeiro, where the Convention on Biological Diversity was established, Conferences of the Parties have been held regularly, and my wife has attended all of them, eventually becoming one of the leading figures in the non-government camp. For example, in 2010 she spent four weeks in Nagoya, attending the pre-conferences, doing several newspaper interviews, and finally attending the conference itself. She is very respected in this area and has spoken with the Japanese Minister of Environment and many other leaders.

IKEDA: Her activities and achievements are indeed impressive. At the Nagoya conference, developed, semi-developed, and developing countries overcame their differences and succeeded in drafting new international rules for the use of biological resources and the protection of ecosystems. This stood out in sharp contrast to the difficult negotiations surrounding the United Nations Framework Convention on Climate Change (UNFCCC or FCCC). These two conventions, established at the 1992 Earth Summit, have often been regarded as twin agreements, but the negotiations concerning the FCCC continue to be especially urgent.

At the seventeenth Conference of the Parties (COP17) to the UN Framework Convention on Climate Change held in Durban, South Africa, in 2011, the Kyoto Protocol was extended to and after 2013, and a schedule was adopted for the establishment of a new framework by 2020, but tough, persistent negotiations based on a recognition of what is truly in the interest of the planet and the human race are needed in order to create an effective framework.

WEIZSÄCKER: The Earth Summit in 1992 was a good and optimistic conference resulting in the adoption of the two major UN conventions on climate (the UN Framework Convention on Climate Change) and on biodiversity (the UN Convention on Biological Diversity) and also of Agenda 21. But ten years later, the 2002 Johannesburg World Summit on Sustainable Development marked a severe backlash. The US delegation, still affected by the shock and subsequent mistrust stirred up by the September 11 terrorist attacks, blocked everything that would result in binding commitments, and the language adopted was all "voluntary." Since Copenhagen in 2009, it is clear that the climate convention is in the doldrums.

My personal assessment of COP16 (2010) is considerably skeptical. One of the most deplorable facts is that Japan, though it was the host country of the Kyoto Protocol, declared that it will not enter into any further Kyoto-based commitments, allowing Canada and Russia, two signatory states of the Kyoto Protocol, to conveniently hide behind Japan and also defer. Following the 2011 COP17 in Durban, South Africa, Canada officially announced that it was withdrawing from the Kyoto Protocol. As such, the prospects remain very dim for a successor protocol binding the industrialized countries to move rapidly ahead and show developing countries the way to low-carbon prosperity. Japan, fortunately, did not follow Canada, so far.

The Green Climate Fund,[4] one of the results of COP16, is meant to be fully established by 2020, but who knows if any private sector sources are going to contribute—and this at a time when government budgets are in deep trouble around the world. The rhetorical support in Cancún for the "2C goal" (not more than 2 degree

Celsius warming over preindustrial levels) is worthless unless firm commitments are made at national and regional levels. One of the few hopes for funding the GCF is the European Union initiative to include air traffic in the EU emissions trading system. But, predictably, the United States and Canada went to the courts to oppose it, seeing their airplanes as exempt from European Union legislation. Fortunately, the European Court denied that indecent exemption.

The only strategy that would have compelled developing countries to join efforts for climatic warming mitigation in a meaningful manner would have been the "per capita equal emission rights approach" or the even more ambitious "budget approach."[5] But neither of the two equity-oriented approaches was even on the negotiating table.

The Durban COP17 intention to arrive at a new protocol by 2020, including newly industrialized countries, may finally open the path for the equity approach. The United States and Canada, in their present mindset, will do everything to block such development, which then rather supports my proposal to create a European-Asian alliance that leaves the United States behind until it develops a new mindset.

GERMANY AND JAPAN

IKEDA: It is true that many unresolved issues remain before us. Experts in various fields are pointing out the need for more fundamental, effective engagement with these problems.

Germany is known as one of the more advanced nations with regard to environmental policies. Its groundbreaking initiatives can be traced back to West Germany, in the period before unification. Starting with the Federal Emission Control Act of 1974, which embodied the philosophy of limiting property rights for the sake of environmental protection, both government policy and public opinion were transformed in the 1970s, leading to widespread support for environmental protection. In 1994, Germany's constitution, the Basic Law for the Federal Republic of Germany, was amended to assign the government the obligation to "protect the natural conditions of life."[6]

I have repeatedly underscored the need for Japan to become an environmental nation. In an article I contributed to a newspaper in Japan, I called for the establishment of a "right to a healthy environment":

> In the twenty-first century, Japan should strive to become a model of advanced environmental protection, including the field of education. It would be appropriate, I believe, to amend Japan's constitution to include a new article protecting the environment. We already have an article in the constitution renouncing war and asserting the right to a peaceful existence, which many countries around the world regard with the highest admiration. While steadfastly preserving our "peace article," adding an article that guarantees the right of human beings to exist in symbiosis with nature would also be very desirable. This principle—the principle of reaching out and forming an alliance with all other human beings on the planet to fulfill our responsibility for the health and happiness of future generations—would be parallel to the principle of peace embodied in Article 9.[7]

In this regard, Japan has much to learn from Germany's pioneering efforts.

WEIZSÄCKER: In the 1970s, Germany definitely learned from Japan regarding environmental problems. Outbreaks of Minamata disease (1950s) and Itai-itai disease (1960s) led Japan to stand out among all nations by establishing strict regulations on heavy metals and on air quality, instigated by the protests of fishermen and also because of the very heavy high atmospheric concentrations of sulfur dioxide and nitrogen oxide at the time.

A good book on Japanese environmental policy as a model for Germany was published in the late 1980s, written by the economist Shigeto Tsuru and Helmut Weidner.[8] It highlighted in particular the long-term approach of Japanese environmental policies, which established ambitious aims but recognized that they would have to be met over a period of ten to fifteen years rather than immediately, thus allowing industry the necessary time to make the changeover loss-free.

In contrast, in Germany—and even more so in America—every few months some new initiative was being undertaken in reaction to a new lawsuit or press campaign. This was absurd. In this regard, in terms of long-term environmental planning by the government, Japan became a model for Germany, and Germany was the follower.

In Japan, industry was forced to pay for sulfur dioxide and nitrous oxide emissions, which led to a rapid cleanup of air quality in once highly polluted regions such as Kansai. In fact, at the time of the Kyoto COP3, Japanese industry had considerably lower carbon dioxide emissions than Germany. This gap became even more dramatic when, at the 1997 COP3 meeting, Germany decided to make 1990, rather than 1997, the base year for calculating its greenhouse gas emission reductions, because 1990 was more or less the peak year of carbon intensity for the German economy, with most of the former GDR (East German) lignite-burning power plants still in operation.

Nevertheless, I agree that Germany is now in a relatively good position in terms of reducing its contribution to climate change and local pollution. Much of the money spent by West Germany to bring East Germany up to speed after the collapse of communism also meant a greening of the relevant industries. And the "Red-Green" coalition government of Chancellor Gerhard Schröder, with its ecological tax reform and EEG (Erneuerbare Energien Gesetz, or Renewable Energy Act), became the leader in the European Union with respect to many aspects of green energy policies.

IKEDA: In the 1950s and '60s, outbreaks of pollution-related Minamata disease, Niigata Minamata disease, Itai-itai disease, and Yokkaichi asthma[9] brought sufferings to many Japanese. In the postwar period, Japanese environmental policy was tied to pollution control. For many years, the majority of pollution control measures have been taken only reluctantly, with a high priority assigned to not obstructing economic growth. Japanese government and industry refused to recognize their responsibility, which significantly extended the suffering of those affected.

In this respect, I think it can be said that Japanese environmental policy has a different point of origin from that of Germany, which is based on making environmental protection a national goal. In Japan, it was the oil shock of the 1970s and the subsequent steep rise in energy prices that initiated efforts to improve energy conservation technology, another sense in which environmental policy in Japan has always been based on finding a balance with economic growth.

Yet, it is probably not true that most Japanese have a low environmental consciousness. As an overview of Japanese history shows, human beings have always been regarded as part of nature, and there is a long tradition of desiring to live in harmony with nature.

WEIZSÄCKER: Germany has an old tradition of seeking to live in harmonious coexistence with nature. The trouble is that much of the tradition was thrown overboard in the postwar period when, following to a large extent the perspective of the Anglo-American worldview, economic growth became the new "god," and greed and selfishness were celebrated as movers of economic growth. Under international pressures, educational systems worldwide have made individual competition for skills the mantra of schools, leaving little space for social cooperation and for integrating humans into nature.

RENEWABLE ENERGY

IKEDA: The approach you cited—the gradual, pragmatic approach of setting long-term goals—is, I believe, the crucial third leg of the tripod, along with transforming the consciousness of each individual and expanding a global consensus, which we must establish in order to solve the global problems we face. With regard to this gradual, pragmatic approach, I am reminded of something Johann Wolfgang von Goethe said to his student Johann Eckermann during their conversations: "The main point is to have a great will, and skill and perseverance to carry it out."[10] And an oft-quoted verse by Goethe contains the lines "Like the stars, without haste, but without rest, let each one go his rounds with his own burden."[11]

I believe that such an indomitable will, persevering conviction, and sense of responsibility and commitment to making the supreme effort to achieve the goal are essential to solve our environmental problems, which will demand an enormous degree of time and work. Finding solutions to our environmental problems resembles, in a way, the negotiations to reduce nuclear arms, also a stubborn problem in which perceived conflicts of national interests often take priority. Speaking of the history of nuclear disarmament, Executive Secretary Tibor Tóth of the Preparatory Commission for the Comprehensive Nuclear-Test-Ban Treaty Organization has said, "The history of disarmament is a process of governments adopting norms and policies only after sustained campaigning from civil society,"[12] attesting to the fact that the people's voices seeking peace were the agents of change. As we have repeatedly confirmed, the ceaseless efforts of citizens' movements are also the key to making the breakthrough for change with regard to environmental issues.

In our previous conversation, you discussed Germany's adoption of renewable energy sources. Germany's focus on offshore wind energy is well known throughout the world, and Germany has also adopted an environmental tax, which has been applied to creating jobs, hasn't it?

WEIZSÄCKER: Since roughly 2005, big hopes have been placed in offshore wind energy. The Scandinavian countries, the United Kingdom, the Netherlands, and Belgium actually built the first large-scale offshore wind parks, and since then, Germany as well as China are also becoming major players in the field. Due to construction challenges and the need for long-distance transmission lines, offshore wind power is estimated to be roughly twice as expensive as onshore wind power.

Germany used the energy tax revenues chiefly to reduce indirect labor costs, such as business contributions to social insurance programs and so forth. This operation seems to have created or secured roughly 250,000 jobs, according to the German Institute for Economic Research.[13] The tax shift made the hiring of people while "firing" kilowatt-hours a profitable operation in many cases. Rising energy prices also induced industry and homeowners to reduce energy consumption, giving jobs to craftsmen for home renovation and to engineers for redesigning industrial processes.

IKEDA: The German experience is valuable not only to Japan but to other countries seeking to shift to renewable energy sources. Germany is generating electricity from a variety of renewable energy sources, with wind turbines in the lead, followed by biomass plants, hydroelectric plants, and photovoltaic sources, in that order.

Denmark was the first to employ wind turbines to generate power. Hans Henningsen, a Danish educator who served as principal of Askov Folk High School, told me that the scientist Poul la Cour experimented with wind power there in 1891.

When I spoke to Mr. Henningsen of the Buddhist view of life— consisting of human beings, nature, and the environment as a whole—and the importance of a symbiotic coexistence between humankind and nature, he said, "Within a Christian context you cannot consider the relation between nature and human beings as something religious in itself"[14] but added that, in light of the Lutheran teaching of the universal presence of God in all things, "there is no point in making a division between the lifeless and the living, . . . or for that matter between things and nature."[15] This observation made a deep impression on me.

The Danish people have a highly developed environmental consciousness. Throughout Europe, there is a general, widespread movement to adopt renewable energy sources.

Renewable energy is not just a means for individual nations to acquire stable energy sources but is also directly linked to preventing climate change on a global scale. UN Human Development Reports have repeatedly sounded the warning that "no one country can win the battle against climate change acting alone. Collective action is not an option but an imperative."[16] As I said earlier, every part of our world is at risk, to a lesser or greater degree, from the abnormal weather patterns and other effects of global climate change (see Conversation Three).

It is absolutely critical for those of us living today to take responsible action for the sake of future generations. What roles, in your opinion, can Japan and Germany play in this regard?

WEIZSÄCKER: My present idea, which I am publicly advocating, is that Europe should join with East Asia, including China, in going ahead with a threefold environmental policy: (1) real climate policy chiefly based on "factor five" technologies; (2) cyclical economy concepts based on the Japanese 3R principle (which was adopted by China in 2009); and (3) the long-term ecological tax reform I have previously outlined, which would make the participating countries pioneers in sustainability technologies.

All developing countries that are poor in energy and other natural resources would be attracted by this new alliance. Europe, East Asia, and the relevant developing countries represent some 80 percent of the world population. If Japan and Germany would initiate a movement in their respective regions for such a new alliance, it would be tremendously exciting and promising, both economically and ecologically.

ETHICAL RESPONSIBILITIES

IKEDA: Japan needs to begin to make comprehensive, systematic efforts to build a sustainable society. I also think it's important for Japan and Germany to share their experience and know-how in this area with other nations in a coordinated fashion.

Based on your many years of experience with environmental issues, what are your thoughts on scientists' ethical responsibilities? With the global environmental issues we face, the scientific community's ethical responsibilities seem to be becoming weightier, don't you think?

WEIZSÄCKER: If you are posing this as an abstract ethical question, then my answer would be *yes*. Scientific and technological advances must be guided by the welfare of society—and nature. But the reality today is that plenty of jobs for scientists are in conventional industry or business stemming from a historical phase of overexploitation of nature. This is the case in the United States and to a slightly lesser extent in Germany and Japan. In many scientific domains, such as biotechnology, you are an outcast if you do not adopt an industrial orientation in your practice of science. This is of course a tragedy but not something that can be changed by moral or ethical exhortations to scientists.

It means that we need to call for ethical responsibility not just from scientists but from the system itself. We need to insist that science be a quest for truth, not profit, and that its results should benefit the public, not restricted commercial interests.

IKEDA: Many of the threats we face today are actually the results of our science and technology. Environmental pollution, for example, is the result of our relentless pursuit of convenience and affluence, which has blinded us to the self-evident principle that we are part of nature and need to live in harmony with it. Nichiren wrote, "As the poisons of greed, anger, and foolishness gradually intensify, the life span of human beings gradually decreases. . . ."[17] The advancement of modern civilization based on science has exacerbated and amplified the greed for possessions and dominance inherent in human beings, until they are on the verge of destroying our natural environment and threatening life itself.

In order to prevent further environmental destruction, it is important to have accurate information regarding the actual severity of the threat constantly presented to the public and to take the necessary legal and policy measures to deal with the problem. Not only experts in the field but the general public must constantly be on the alert and monitoring the actions taken by government and business.

WEIZSÄCKER: Precisely. If the sciences are about truth, they cannot avoid looking at the effects of science and technology. When a scientist develops a pharmaceutical agent, he or she should feel obliged to investigate its side effects, both the benign and the harmful ones. A lack of such curiosity can mean overlooking the possibility of terrible side effects. It is therefore not justified to define "good science" as narrow fact-finding within one's own discipline.

Technologies have typically been financed and further developed if they carried the prospect of some further expansion of desires and convenience, because that would make them successful in the market. Scientists and engineers, like other human beings, have a tendency to do what they are being paid for. We can't blame them for that. Teachers, priests, and craftsmen are also paid for what they do. But once we realize that further conventional economic expansion is no longer benign, and that contraction is necessary to save what remains of climate stability and biodiversity, we ought to think of new avenues for science and technology.

If we manage to extract five times more human well-being from a kilowatt-hour or a bucket of fresh water, we can theoretically provide pleasant lives and convenience to one billion people in the rich countries with one-fifth of today's energy and water consumption and also offer a fivefold increase of economic wealth to people in the poor countries without increasing their energy and water consumption. Scientists learning about such opportunities tend to become excited and engaged in finding practical ways to make them a reality. This has been my daily experience at the Wuppertal Institute for Climate, Environment and Energy. The next important step is to reflect on the institutional conditions needed to make such fabulous improvements truly profitable.

IKEDA: Concerning scientists' responsibility, Dr. Rotblat told me that while many scientists take no responsibility for how their scientific discoveries are employed, he considered this a fundamentally immoral stance. He added:

> The world's scientists can make a definitive statement
> about the application of scientific knowledge in society

because they have had such an immense impact on people's lives and have played a major role in shaping contemporary society.[18]

Dr. Rotblat was an advocate of the need for scientists to have a strong moral conscience and an awareness of their mission as scientists.

I am also reminded of something that the father of modern chemistry and great peace activist Linus Pauling said to me:

> Since I believe in democracy, I prefer to see no single group—not even scientists—running the world. Scientists have an obligation to help their fellow citizens understand what the problems are but must not form a controlling oligarchy. Decisions must be made by the people as a whole.[19]

It is important, I believe, for scientists to work with civil society in order to build a healthy society.

It is equally important for institutes of higher learning, in order to foster astute, capable young minds with an abiding sense of social responsibility, to provide an education with high moral values. This is why I want to ask if you would offer a few words of encouragement not only to the students of Soka University, which you once visited, but to all the women and men dedicating themselves to the invaluable task of learning in their youth.

WEIZSÄCKER: Soka University contrasts with other universities in that it has not allowed itself to be incorporated into the Wall Street mindset. It aims at providing its students with a firm intellectual foundation and encourages them to examine and cultivate an understanding of history, religion, and morals. This I find to be very positive.

My general impression is that Soka University generously

cultivates liberal and interdisciplinary approaches, reminding me of the great days of German universities during the nineteenth century, based on the liberal arts and science principles of Wilhelm von Humboldt.[20] I regret to say that these virtues have been gradually sacrificed and replaced by a narrow focus by students on career preparation and by faculties on highly specialized methodological scholastics. I wish to congratulate Soka University for following a broader road.

My personal message to young people is to be intellectually hungry, bold, and responsible.

The Long-term Perspective

IKEDA: Allow me to reiterate my congratulations to you, Dr. Weizsäcker, on your selection as a co-president of the Club of Rome at the Annual Conference in Bucharest, hosted by the Romanian Association of the Club of Rome in October 2012. Your appointment surely attests to the high esteem in which you are held for your invaluable contributions to the Club of Rome over many years, as well as your distinguished body of groundbreaking research on environmental issues. My fellow members in Germany and in the 192 countries and territories in which the SGI is established join me in offering our sincere congratulations.

WEIZSÄCKER: I would like to thank you for the congratulatory telegram you sent when I was selected for the post. I will do my best to serve in this position, together with co-president and former member of the European Parliament Anders Wijkman.

It is absolutely necessary for the Club of Rome to have new ideas and new working topics, maintaining an image that is coherent with the earlier profile of the Club and at the same time offering new perspectives for the future. The earlier profile of the Club of Rome was essentially a warning; the new profile should present opportunities as well, linked to the specific warnings of *The Limits to Growth*.

IKEDA: The Annual Conference in 2012 marked the fortieth anniversary of the publication of the Club of Rome's first report, *The Limits to Growth*, reinforcing the conference's significance as a fresh departure toward the attainment of sustainable growth. *The Limits to Growth* compellingly argues:

> He (Man) has all that is physically necessary to create a totally new form of human society—one that would be built to last for generations. The two missing ingredients are a realistic, long-term goal that can guide mankind to the equilibrium society and the human will to achieve that goal. . . . With that goal and that commitment, mankind would be ready now to begin a controlled, orderly transition from growth to global equilibrium.[1]

We of the SGI hope that the Club of Rome will continue to articulate a vision of a sustainable global society from the perspective of the human race as a whole and to assume leadership in shaping public opinion. We hold the highest expectations for your success, Dr. Weizsäcker, as an insightful, widely admired leader of the organization. As an honorary member, I am determined to do my best, however modest my contributions may be, to work with and support you and the Club's distinguished members.

Studies reveal that every year, worldwide, 13 million acres of forest—an area equal to one-seventh that of Japan—are lost.[2] In many countries, water tables continue to drop, causing chronic water shortages, and it is estimated that almost 25 percent of the planet's land area is affected by desertification.[3]

Against this backdrop, in June 2012, the UN Conference on Sustainable Development (Rio+20) was held in Rio de Janeiro. At the Japan Pavilion near the main venue of the conference, the SGI presented the exhibition *Seeds of Hope: Visions of Sustainability, Steps Toward Change* (cosponsored by the City of Rio de Janeiro and Earth Charter International, and supported by Rio de Janeiro State), and in coordination, I offered (on June 5, 2012) an environmental proposal, "For a Sustainable Global Society: Learning for Empowerment and Leadership."[4]

I have heard that you co-chaired the International Resource Panel of the UN Environment Programme as well as played a role in other side events, and that you also spoke on the panel. Governmental officials and representatives of companies and NGOs from all over the world took part in Rio+20, which attracted massive attention, bringing to the fore numerous issues.

WEIZSÄCKER: During the conference, with regard to promoting the green economy, there was a divide between North and South: The North and UNEP advocated the shift to a green economy, while the South rejected that approach as a pretext for protectionism on the part of the more developed economies—a claim with which I cannot agree.

At least the official conference agreed to stick to the Rio Principles of 1992, to allow for technology assessment at the UN level and to make a step toward strengthening the UNEP. Otherwise, some new ideas were found outside the official conference, at side events.

I was chairing one with former prime minister of Norway Harlem Brundtland and former president of Chile Michelle Bachelet, now the chief of UN Women (United Nations Entity for Gender Equality and the Empowerment of Women).[5] The event was attended by the executive director of UNICEF, the general secretary of the International Trade Union Confederation, and other luminaries. Consensus was expressed concerning such issues as care for future generations, the fate of children today, the correct balance between women and men, and other important matters. This is just one example, I think, of the positive results emerging from side events.

LESSONS FROM RIO+20

IKEDA: It's important to reinforce the fresh ideas that emerged from the side events and develop them further.

Among the achievements of Rio+20 that you cited, there is one that has shown immediate progress—the strengthening of the UNEP. At the meeting of the UN General Assembly held in December 2012, steps were taken to fortify UNEP, including the adoption of a resolution to open UNEP's Governing Council to all nations, extending universal membership. This is a significant step, I believe, and one I stressed as an important element of needed institutional reforms in my 2008 peace proposal and June 2012 environmental proposal, as the adoption of universal membership allows all interested nations to take part in the council's decisions and actions.

Harlem Brundtland is an eminent authority on environmental issues, widely recognized for her work with the World Commission on Environment and Development, also known as the Brundtland Commission. When the SGI held its *War and Peace* exhibition in Oslo, Norway, in 1991, our representatives paid a courtesy visit to Ms. Brundtland, who was then prime minister, and she responded with a personal message. Moreover, Michelle Bachelet, the first woman president of Chile, led the rebuilding efforts following the great earthquake in her country in 2010. President Bachelet has been working to improve the status and rights of women, and it goes without saying that the empowerment of women is absolutely indispensable for attaining a sustainable society.

The SGI focuses on each individual's empowerment and thus cosponsored a side event at the Rio+20 Conference, "The Future We Create: an interdisciplinary roundtable on the role of education and learning toward a sustainable future" (cosponsored by the Centre for Environment Education, the UN Commission on Sustainable Development Education Caucus, Human Rights Education Associates, and Inter Press Service). Five international experts in various fields who had been involved in promoting education in civil society took part and engaged in a lively discussion.

Pam Puntenney, co-chair of the CSD Education Caucus, noted that in an age of such dramatic, sudden change, today's conventions will no longer apply tomorrow. She urged us to stop clinging to the methods of the past and instead develop new institutions and reassess outdated modes of thought. She further stressed the importance of education that fosters leadership over conformity, so that through education, every person can change the world.[6]

The theme of the roundtable, "The Future We Create," carried the theme of Rio+20, "The Future We Want," one step further. I have been told that the conference was characterized by the determination to foster protagonists who will help resolve humanity's present plight and form alliances within civil society.

What other thoughts or reactions did you have based on your participation in Rio+20?

WEIZSÄCKER: Well, many at the conference were critical of the present dominance of the financial markets. Clearly, human ethics should not be steered by profits. Justice and other public goods should be managed by democratically legitimate states, not by anonymous financial markets. A current tragedy is that markets tend to undercut the ability of states to create anything like equality. There are environmental groups who do good things on a local level in a way that prevents markets from interfering, but most of the groups participating in the side events are just too weak to change the brutal game that financial markets play with states.

I believe that more than 99 percent of the daily international monetary trade has no immediate basis in goods and services. It is just the movement of money, meaning speculation. In effect, it is also speculating with the fate of our grandchildren, speculating with the fate of poor people in Angola, speculating with the banks in Spain, speculating with the planet's environment and climate. All these are being subjected to speculation.

This mindset would not allow states to interfere with markets. To me, this is madness, but this is the dominant mindset of the world today.

IKEDA: This is why the markets are often decried as just a "money game." Just like the recent financial crisis—triggered by unbridled, overheated speculation—the environmental destruction spreading rapidly across the globe is caused by prioritizing economic growth and reflects this vicious cycle of unchecked human greed.

Brazil, the scene of Rio+20, is home to the world's largest rainforest, the Amazon, which is steadily being destroyed. At our Rio+20 side event, the initiatives of Brazil SGI's Amazon Ecological Conservation Center[7] roused considerable interest. Having greeted its twentieth anniversary in 2012, the center, which is located in Manaus, the State of Amazonas, was built on wasteland from which the original forest had been cleared. In an attempt to redress through human action the environmental ruin wrought by human action, we adopted enrichment tree planting, a reforestation method that relies on a mixed planting of useful trees without damaging the forest as it regenerates. Today, 20,000 trees of sixty species have been planted in the area, where birds and animals of many species live. In recognition of this effort, Brazil's Ministry of Environment and the Brazilian Institute of Environment and

Renewable Natural Resources have designated the area a Private Natural Heritage Reserve.

In an effort to ensure the long-term protection of the Amazon basin, the center has sponsored environmental education programs for the local people, who previously had no opportunities to learn about the Amazon River and the Amazon Rainforest. The center invites dozens of public school students at a time in an effort to encourage comprehensive environmental awareness, focusing on a three-step process I proposed on the occasion of the 2002 World Summit on Sustainable Development in South Africa: encouraging people to learn, to reflect, and to empower themselves. For example, after studying about local fish in the classroom, the students go to the river and catch fish to study before releasing them again. The students also go into the forest and observe how the trees they planted are growing. To date, a total of some 20,000 students have taken part in the program. In addition, the center has joined hands with surrounding communities to promote environmental initiatives such as recycling.

WEIZSÄCKER: To the extent that I know it, I have highest admiration for what you and the SGI are doing, including in Brazil. There are many other groups doing wonderful things, efforts that can be likened to oases for the survival of humankind in a desert of destruction. It is absolutely essential to have some oasis structures to protect humanity and nature from destruction.

Today, hundreds of billions of euros and dollars and trillions of yen are spent in subsidies for destruction, and the international capital markets reward the quarterly reports of firms who maximize profit by harvesting faster than nature's renewal. This is one modus operandi of international business today. Business quarterly reports are the symbol of economic short-termism, which is the opposite, by definition, of conservation and sustainability in the long-term. The real costs of this short-term outlook have to be identified and analyzed. That could help rebalance public with private goods.

My decision, in 1997, to run for a seat in parliament was in a sense motivated by such considerations. Chairing the parliamentary Select Committee on Globalization was a privileged learning situation for me and enhanced my determination to work on the priority of public goods and a long-term outlook.

I am full of admiration for those who work so hard to create little local oases, but I watch with a sense of tragedy, of sorrow and melancholy, as I see many of those wonderful, excellent, local attempts being overwhelmed by the maelstrom of rent-seeking international capital. And while the Brazilian government no doubt appreciates the Brazil SGI initiative for the Amazon Ecological Conservation Center, it has in the meantime continued to destroy a large area of forest each month. So, for all my sympathy with all those admirable and well-meaning activities, I believe the people of the world will have to stand up against destructive structures by building and supporting international and national legislation.

IKEDA: As you say, we need to strengthen policies to protect public goods based on the long-term perspective. The Amazon basin is a treasure chest of biodiversity, home to more than ten million species. SGI Brazil is continuing its courageous struggle to preserve the Amazon basin as a shining hope for the preservation of our planet's biodiversity.

The Lotus Sutra, which presents the essence of the Buddhist teachings, contains a famous passage: "Jeweled trees abound in flowers and fruit where living beings enjoy themselves at ease."[8] The message is that treasuring our natural environment is indispensable for enabling the sanctity of life to shine brightly. We of the SGI are determined to reach out to like-minded individuals and expand the effort to protect the "jeweled trees" sparkling with life in all their diversity.

Other Energy Options

Ikeda: Next, I want to discuss the energy problem, which is of course deeply connected to the environment. In my peace proposal submitted in January 2012, in which I offered my thoughts on the global energy issue, I stressed that it was imperative, from the perspective of sustainability, that Japan seriously consider shifting to an energy policy not dependent on nuclear power. I also said that Japan should adopt as its mission collaboration with other countries, spearheading efforts to introduce renewable energy sources, co-developing ways to achieve substantial energy cost reductions while promoting technological innovation that will facilitate the introduction of renewable energy sources in developing countries currently struggling with energy issues.[9]

In Conversation One, we discussed Germany's push to wean itself from nuclear power generation and how this effort has accelerated in earnest since 2011. What plans are under way to replace the power capacity currently generated by nuclear plants, and how will the shift to other forms of energy be executed?

Weizsäcker: The official plan is for Germany to phase out nuclear power generation completely by 2022. The official discourse speaks of invigorating the growth of wind energy and solar power generation, but clandestine planning is under way to resort to fossil fuels to generate almost the same amount of electricity that is to be lost in dismantling nuclear power generating facilities. This doesn't receive much public attention, but it's a reality, and the government's justification is that it is replacing old-fashioned coal-powered plants with integrated gasification combined cycle power plants, which are more efficient and less carbon intensive. This, however, is not a long-term solution.

The efficiency side of the equation, which is in my view by far the most important, is still badly neglected. Renewable energy technologies, of course, are flourishing. They need new infrastructures to make up for geographical differences and meteorological fluctuations. One topic is new high-voltage power transmission lines to bring the electricity produced by offshore wind in the North Sea to southern Germany, but these are problems that can be solved.

What is missing is the creation of smart grids, of efficiency legislation, and of an active policy of overcoming the wasteful age of cheap energy. We need to reduce subsidies on energy use and perhaps agree on a "corridor" of energy prices predictably moving upward, more or less in parallel with efficiency gains, so that monthly costs for energy services remain essentially stable while steadily increasing the incentive to become more energy efficient.

IKEDA: With regard to promoting renewable energy sources, the Act on Special Measures concerning the Procurement of Renewable Electric Energy by Operators of Electric Utilities went into effect in July 2012. Under this Act, Japan has begun to adopt Feed-in Tariffs, which mandate the buyback of electric power generated from renewable sources and thus encourages investment in renewable energy technologies.[10]

A power feed-in law, the Stromeinspeisungsgesetz, was adopted in 1991 in Germany (see earlier discussion in Conversation Three). This was followed in 2000 by Germany's Renewable Energy Act, which, in several subsequent amendments, has furthered the policy of feed-in tariffs. When the policy of feed-in tariffs in Germany, a global pioneer in this area, was adopted, you were active on Germany's political stage.

WEIZSÄCKER: I was a member of parliament when we adopted the Feed-in Tariff Law in 2000. It was a very important achievement for German democracy. It was done by parliament, initially against the wish of the Ministry for Economic Affairs and Energy. One member of parliament, my friend, Hermann Scheer, had taken the initiative to table a bill. Then, we had a formal debate in the parliamentary caucus of the Social Democrats on the draft bill, and after a discussion of an hour or two, we had an 80 percent majority in favor. A very similar thing happened in the Green Party caucus. Next, there were the first, second, and third readings in parliament, and the bill was adopted. Chancellor Schröder, who initially expressed hesitation, fully accepted the vote and later advertised and promoted it as "his law."

The main reason for the law's success was that those feeding in renewable electricity were compensated for all their costs, even if the costs were very high, particularly for photovoltaics (solar power). At the time, photovoltaic power was very expensive, up to two Deutschmarks per kilowatt-hour. So, it was an expensive law, but it was not funded by the national budget. It was the electricity users who had to pay. Industry, as usual, got away with exemptions, as some companies were threatening to leave Germany if they had to pay full costs. I believe that it was crucial that they received them in this case.

The European Commissioner for Competition, however, rejected the exemptions for industry, calling them market-distorting subsidies. But some compromise was found, and hardly any company left the country. The law guaranteed stability for investors in renewable energies—that was the core of the law. This caused a huge upswing in wind energy development. The law was copied by fifty different nations around the world, including China.

With the growth in renewable energy, the compensation it

mandated in the form of feed-in tariffs became ever more costly, and it was eventually necessary to reduce the feed-in tariffs. This was acceptable, however, because the costly pioneer investments in renewable energy had by that time already been made; later investments are a lot cheaper. Even with the reduced tariffs, the principle that they should be cost-covering was maintained. When costs drop, tariffs can drop, too.

IKEDA: This is extremely useful information for the formulation of Japan's energy policy. Of course, the circumstances in Germany and Japan, starting with their geography, are quite different, but at this point, where we in Japan are just embarking on a feed-in tariffs system, there are heightened expectations for the renewable energy sector. The installation of photovoltaic equipment is being promoted for private homes, and a growing number of commercial plans for mega-solar farms, as well as wind and geothermal power generation facilities, are underway across Japan.

We are now searching for ways to produce energy appropriate to the special characteristics of each region of Japan, under the auspices of promoting local energy self-sufficiency to strengthen regional autonomy. The consumption of locally produced power has the added benefit of avoiding the enormous losses that occur with long-distance power transmission, leading to more efficient use of energy. Such thinking may already be commonplace in Germany, but in Japan, it represents new hope for a better future.

WEIZSÄCKER: I believe regional energy self-sufficiency is a lot easier in Germany than in Japan, for geographical reasons. For example, the small municipality of Freiamt, not far from my hometown of Emmendingen, is energy self-sufficient. They produce more local power than they need and can export it. And the *land* (state) Schleswig-Holstein seems to produce five times more wind energy than its typical electricity consumption. But Freiamt is a rural village, and rural Schleswig-Holstein is blessed with a lot of wind. So their situations are not comparable with those of large and densely populated urban areas such as Nagoya or Tokyo.

I would not recommend biomass energy production in Japan, because you need to use all existing fertile land for agriculture; even in Germany, biomass energy production is cutting into food supplies, and it's even worse in America.

Photovoltaics can be a very good energy source in Japan. They are becoming more efficient both in terms of cost and in terms of yield per square meter. So with even relatively modest-sized buildings—for example, the type that are found in suburban Japan—you can have energy self-sufficiency from solar power alone.

Geothermal power also has a lot of potential for Japan. There are two types of geothermal energy production. One employs a heat pump, which is installed underground, below a house, for example. Though this kind of pump runs on electricity, you can extract much more energy than you invest. This is readily accessible, small-scale, geothermal energy production.

The other type is tapping deep geothermal energy from hard, dry rock. That is costly and only possible under certain conditions, such as those found in Iceland and the Philippines. It may be practical in certain places in Japan as well, where the heat source is only a few hundred meters or so below surface. All in all, the prospect for renewable energy may be more difficult in Japan than in other countries, making the energy efficiency agenda even more important in Japan than in Germany or Brazil. Reducing the demand for energy should be the main focus in Japan.

IKEDA: Since the March 2011 earthquake and tsunami, there has been increased awareness in Japan that our country is one of the world's leading nations in its potential to produce geothermal power. There has also been greater focus on promoting renewable energy and improving energy-saving technologies. Energy-saving technologies and energy conservation are great ways to reduce energy consumption, but you have also highlighted the issue of how we use energy.

In February 2012, you attended an international symposium at Nagoya University, "Climate Change, Resource-Energy Use and Sustainability of the Earth and Human Society." I read a digest of your speech on that occasion.[11] To seriously tackle energy conservation, you described how the production of a cup of strawberry yogurt in Germany requires ingredients that must be shipped nearly 5,000 miles. Clearly, this example prompts us all to reexamine how we now operate.

WEIZSÄCKER: So far, very little has been done in Germany in this regard. The dairy firms producing strawberry yogurt did absolutely the right things in terms of business management by reducing labor and shipping the products long-distance in trucks over the road system. The roads, of course, were available free of charge to the trucks, so their cost does not appear in the cost of shipping. That made the 5,000-mile crisscrossing of Europe perfectly rational in business terms. Of course, it is not elegant.

Germany, like the United States and others, had a false understanding of the Japanese just-in-time philosophy.[12] This was invented in Japan, where you had the main factory—for instance, Toyota in Aichi—with small suppliers in the immediate vicinity, very short distances away. The Germans and others thought the same model should be applied to German automakers, such as Volkswagen in Wolfsburg, but with suppliers often located as far as Portugal or Poland. As a result, German manufacturers had to resort to large-scale, long-distance transport, which is not ecologically sustainable.

Now, we can turn to politics again. Imagine that with a predictable, gradual increase of energy prices, including gas, the distances for the supply chain would gradually shrink, perhaps down to the typical Japanese dimensions.

IKEDA: In pursuing further energy savings, we cannot stop at simply reducing the environmental burden we place on our environment but must strive to open the way to creating a sustainable global society. To build a better society for future generations, we need to not only summon all the wisdom at our disposal but also act wisely and build a broad network of solidarity.

Environmental Awareness

IKEDA: Described as a "teacher of humanity," Shakyamuni expressed his profound compassion by declaring, "Seen or unseen, those dwelling far or near, those who are born or those who are to be born, may all beings be happy!"[1] "All beings" is not limited to humans but includes all living things equally. The wish "may all beings be happy" embraces those beings currently alive and those yet to be born—all life in the past, present, and future.

I believe that this perspective is intimately connected with the concept of sustainability. This spirit of coexistence, based on the awareness that we human beings are part of nature and the wish for the happiness of self and others alike, is assuming even greater urgency in today's global society. With the rapid advancement of globalization, as various problems are compounded and mutually exacerbated, resulting in dire global consequences, it is crucial to think deeply about the precious dignity of life and to base our actions and our lifestyle choices on careful consideration of what facets of our societies we cannot afford to sacrifice, what we must preserve for the future.

Based on your commitment to build a sustainable society, you have lectured around the world and engaged in a wide range of activities to raise public awareness of environmental issues. In March 2010, you gave a special public lecture and participated as keynote speaker in a symposium sponsored by the Institute of Oriental Philosophy, which I founded.

Symposium participants commented that they gained a renewed appreciation for the establishment of an ethical foundation for sustainable development and the need for scientific and technological contributions to overcome threats to the global environment. I thank you again for your participation in the symposium. Individual citizens' awareness and deepening understanding of the global environment can become important forces to solve environmental problems.

WEIZSÄCKER: I do believe that teaching the reality of the world's ongoing destruction and of the mechanisms that are responsible for this destruction are very important and potentially helpful. In addition, teaching how people can lead happy lives without destroying the environment—be it in Bhutan or in Japan or Germany—can also be helpful, because such examples stir positive emotions and make people receptive to the idea of sustainable lifestyles.

Providing information is especially important. For example, a student who has learned about sustainable lifestyles may be impressed and share his excitement with a classmate. That classmate may respond: "Don't be a fool. Why give up the riches available to you? What good is that?" The idealistic student needs ammunition to rebut such cynicism, ammunition in the form of solid information.

In such cases, it's not enough to reply with vague, mystical, or quasi-religious assertions. They are unlikely to be convincing. The student needs to be able to answer concretely and practically, based on reality. That's more effective as education and spreading the message.

IKEDA: Correct understanding and recognition of reality are important. They are the foundation that engenders correct actions and lifestyle choices by each individual to build a sustainable society.

In this sense, starting from childhood, people need opportunities for environmental education in which, through actual experiences, they can become familiar with the wonders of the natural environment and learn about its condition. There are countries today that have instituted regular school courses in environmental science and nature.

As just one example of these programs, students at the Kansai Soka Junior and Senior High Schools are taking part in the NASA (the US National Aeronautics and Space Administration) Earth-Kam program.[2] The students remotely operate a camera installed on the International Space Station in orbit about 250 miles above the Earth, and take photographs of our planet. Since their initial participation in 2000, they have carried out analysis and research of the photos, centered around topics of their own choosing. They are also conducting weather observations of locations around the globe to study the effects of climate change. Through these activities, the students gain a renewed awareness of our planet's beauty while at the same time witness with their own eyes the loss of forests, increasing desertification, and other forms of environmental degradation, thus raising their consciousness of environmental issues.

In 1971, the West German government established the Environmental Programme to formalize environmental education starting at the elementary school level. This and the Programme for Environmental Protection of the same year became pillars of Germany's environmental policy and attracted worldwide attention.

One positive result, as recorded in a revised edition of the Japanese-language publication of the German consulates in Osaka and Kobe, *Kankyo senshinkoku doitsu* (Advanced Environmental Nation Germany), was as follows:

> The number of "eco-warriors" who received environmental education at the elementary school level continues to increase, and since the 1980s they have grown into an important core in the formation of public opinion to date.[3]

Fostering young people with a high degree of environmental awareness is the surest, most important pathway to build a sustainable society, I believe.

As a university professor and president, you were an important contributor to German education in the 1970s, the dawn of German environmental education. What are your thoughts on the efforts for environmental education in Germany up to the present?

WEIZSÄCKER: I'm not sure I can fully answer your question, but in German schools, learning has traditionally been—and to a large extent still is—highly compartmentalized. There is Latin, or in older schools, Ancient Greek, which of course, like Latin, no one speaks. There is mathematics, physics, chemistry, biology, and so forth. There are no courses on the environment and none on the economy. As a result, there are periodic uprisings of criticism of the educational system. Some say that Ancient Greek should be dropped and economics taught. Others say classical physics should be replaced by computer science, or that foreign language instruction should be replaced by video courses. Over the years, many such calls for the modernization of the German educational system have arisen.

One such call for change took place in the 1970s, when it was proposed that environmental education be added to the curriculum. It would have removed the barriers separating biology, chemistry, physics, and geography, and combined them all in the study of the environment. The effect of this call for reform was, however, quite limited. Actually, newspapers, television, and direct experience have been much more influential than the schools in providing environmental education.

As far as good books for environmental education, I can recommend one by a friend of mine, the retired journalist Dietrich Jörn Weder: *Umwelt: Bedrohung und Bewahrung* (Environment: Threats and Conservation).[4] It's good, well illustrated, and insightful.

EMPOWERED CHILDREN

IKEDA: It's important to carry out environmental education not just at school but through promoting direct interaction and involvement with the environment at the community level. In the book you mentioned, Weder writes, "Only the human race can sever the root of the world, and it is probably in the process of doing so."[5] I believe that now is the time for us to shift from a society of mass production, mass consumption, and mass waste to a sustainable society. In addition, as I said before, it is crucial to foster the younger generation to carry on and accelerate this trend.

Earlier, I cited the term "eco-warrior" in reference to environmental education in Germany. Today, more and more people are coming to regard children not so much as needing protection from a variety of threats but as agents for change and reform, capable of stirring a groundswell for transformation in their families, communities, and society—a stance many UN institutions have taken.

I am reminded of a particular incident—something that former UN Under-Secretary-General Anwarul K. Chowdhury shared in a dialogue with me. While working at the UN Headquarters, he recounted, there was a serious water shortage in New York. New York's mayor at the time, Edward Irving "Ed" Koch, appointed all

the city's young students as "deputy mayors for water conservation." He gave them buttons proclaiming their new responsibilities, which included monitoring and supervising water usage at
home to prevent waste. The children, proud of their important
mission, carried it out with great seriousness, Mr. Chowdhury
said. His own son was one of the "deputy mayors," allowing his
father just four minutes to shower. If he inadvertently went over
the time limit, his son banged on the bathroom door, telling him
his time was up and ordering him to turn the water off.[6] In the end,
the mayor's program was a great success.

This demonstrates how important it is to build a mass movement to solve our global environmental problems. We need to
awaken not just adults but children to society's problems and find
creative ways to instill sound values in them regarding our environmental resources.

WEIZSÄCKER: My observation is that, historically, education typically follows rather than creates the zeitgeist, the mindset of the
time. When Ronald Reagan and Margaret Thatcher and Augusto
Pinochet came in with a new ideology of markets, you saw all
the schools of the world teaching markets, markets, markets! And
before that, when the big environmental debate took place in the
late 1960s—triggered by ecologist Rachel Carson in America; by
Willy Brandt in Germany in 1961, with his slogan, *"Blauer Himmel
über der Ruhr"* (Restore Blue Skies Over the Ruhr!); and in Japan
with the uproar over Minamata and Itai-itai diseases—everybody
was in a state of alarm over the environment. In reaction, you
saw schools all over the world teaching about the environment.
It was not the other way around: Rachel Carson didn't become
a pioneering environmental reformer because she studied about
the environment at school. For all the merits of good education,
my empirical observation is that education follows the mindset
of the time.

As a result, my interest is in changing that mindset, so that it then becomes easier for education ministries, for schools, for pupils, for parents, and for teachers to do what is good for their grandchildren. Today, unfortunately, many are doing just the opposite. That said, I agree that it is important to improve environmental education through every possible channel—the media, television, the schools, and every other means.

If you look at the discussion in Germany about the so-called failings of German education revealed by the PISA (Program for International Student Assessment) of the Organization for Economic Co-operation and Development, we are learning exactly the wrong lesson from the results of the assessment. In Germany, the focus of education was relatively philosophical and relaxed, but now that the PISA results have shown that German students are behind, for example, the Koreans and the Chinese in mathematics, there is a great drive to force our pupils into excelling at mathematics.

Exactly the same thing happened in the United States. I mean, America was the home of the great philosopher John Dewey, a nature lover, people lover, and a great pedagogue. And American education, embodying many of Dewey's ideas, became the basis for the humanitarian courage of the United States to stand up against fascism—against German fascism, against Japanese militarism, against Soviet communism. Much that we love about America is rooted in John Dewey, but Dewey's educational model is currently being replaced by mathematization, statistics, and the adoration of the media and the Internet.

Our Ecological Footprints

IKEDA: Education needs to cultivate a mindset based on a fair, balanced, and expansive perspective rather than one distorted by a particular doctrine or dogma.

Makiguchi, the founder of Soka (Value-creating) education, was an impassioned critic of Japan's rigid educational system, insisting that the teacher's role is not to cram information into pupils' heads but to richly foster their creativity and humanity, ingraining in them a way of life dedicated to enabling themselves and others to become happy. He stressed the need to transform education from a means of inculcating service to the nation and advancing political, military, economic, ideological, and other national goals, to a means of contributing to children's happiness and maximizing the student's full potential as a complete person. Makiguchi was drawn to Dewey's educational philosophy; the two shared a common belief that education should facilitate and further the recognition that we are all citizens of the world.

Changing the mindset of the times, as you put it, can also be described as establishing a broad, new social ethic, including this underpinning education. In this context, I want to discuss the best way to raise public consciousness.

Goethe, himself a global citizen, said in his last years, "Let everyone sweep in front of his own door, and the whole world will be clean."[7] This hallowed wisdom—if we all observe our proper duties and take care of our immediate environment, everything will go smoothly—remains an ethical truism on the individual level today. It is also an ethos of good citizenship, affirming that if each citizen carries out his or her own duties and responsibilities, society as a whole will benefit.

But is it sufficient today to merely clean up our immediate surroundings, and how are we to dispose of the resulting garbage? While such questions would no doubt provoke a rueful smile from Goethe, that we must be attuned to such larger issues attests to the difficulty of living in this day and age, facing as we do a global environmental crisis.

We need to think about what happens to what we sweep from our doorway even after it is no longer in sight. It is a time in which the naïve optimism that we can leave our garbage to nature's capacity to recycle and restore things is no longer acceptable. This is a domain involving industrial structures and economic activity, public and private behaviors and ethics, and environmental awareness, among numerous other factors.

What standards of conduct do you think individual citizens need to observe in this century of the environment?

WEIZSÄCKER: Well, our family tries to get our food from mostly local farmers and the most ecologically responsible sources. We have just one car for a family of eight people, and we try to do our longer trips by rail. I, however, have to fly to Japan, Rio de Janeiro, California, and so forth, so my ecological footprint is much too big. In my defense, I cannot teach students in Japan or California from my home in Emmendingen.

In Goethe's time, the actual geographical reach of a person, whether farmer, laborer, or bourgeois, was essentially the immediate area outside their doors. Today, in contrast, 95 percent of my ecological footprint is in Malaysia, Siberia, Canada, Saudi Arabia, and Japan. We have outsourced the problem. The true contemporary reach of Goethe's "space in front of our doorsteps" has been rendered invisible, because it is somewhere on the other side of the globe. What we need to do now is make our ecological footprints transparent, revealing just how big that space in front of our doorstep actually is.

Both Germany and Japan have been pioneers in exporting the problem. The Japanese in the 1970s made energy more expensive in Japan. It was good for Japan. It triggered a lot of innovation—for example, the digital revolution in cameras and numerous other developments—but at the same time, Japan exported its aluminum industry to Indonesia, to Siberia, to Brazil, and other places.

What we need to do now is restore the visibility of our personal environmental destruction and ecological footprint so that we can see it, and also put a price tag on it.

IKEDA: As with the ecological footprint, the dividends from numerically quantifying the burden human beings place on the environment are significant. Previously, I introduced the three stages I proposed for environmental education (see Conversation Five). Learning of the burden we place on the environment corresponds to the first step of "learning." This is, I think, the gateway to environmental education. The ecological footprint is, simply put, the area of land and water required to support one human life.[8]

According to the *Living Planet Report 2012* of the WWF, the Earth's total biocapacity in 2008 was 12 billion gha (global hectare, the average biocapacity of all hectare measurements of biologically productive areas on the planet), while humanity's ecological footprint was 18.2 billion gha, or 1.5 times what the Earth can produce and absorb in a single year.[9] On a per capita basis, the Earth's capacity is 1.8 gha per person, and we are using 2.7 gha per person. In other words, the demands of our present lifestyle on our planet far exceed the finite resources available. The report goes on to say that should this situation continue, by 2030, even two planet Earths will not be enough to support the human race.[10]

By understanding the true toll of our ecological footprint in this way and realizing how much of the Earth's resources we are actually consuming, we can move on to the next step in environmental education: reflecting on our lifestyles, which is directly linked to the third stage in the process, empowering ourselves to take concrete action to change our lifestyles.

A NEW ENLIGHTENMENT

IKEDA: I want to discuss the Japanese attitude toward the environment. In our previous discussions, you have said that the 3Rs, the core concepts for a recycling society—reducing waste, reusing finite resources, and recycling what we can—originated in Japan. As in so many places around the world with a long history of farming, fishing, animal husbandry, and forestry, a hallowed spiritual tradition of working in harmony with nature has developed in local communities in Japan.

Research shows that even the great metropolis of Edo, Japan's capital from the seventeenth century, was an ecologically minded city that employed the wisdom of recycling systems. In the Edo period, this was motivated not so much by the current desire to reduce disposable waste as the ethos of valuing all resources and making the best use of them.

For example, oil pressed from grape, camellia, and sesame seeds was used as fuel for lanterns, while the leftover meal was employed as fertilizer. Rice straw was used to make straw sandals, rope, and other objects of daily use, and was burned as fuel.[11] There were also merchants who specialized in collecting and recycling paper scraps, worn-out clothing, and even ashes, indicating that there was little actual waste in Edo society, truly a recycling society based on the 3Rs.

However, with the sudden wave of modernization accompanying industrialization and the enormous population shift to urban areas, traditional communities disappeared, their hallowed wisdom lost its relevance or was eventually forgotten, and their spirit of harmonious coexistence with nature was gradually ignored. This conflict between tradition and modernism is taking place all around the world.

Of course, we should concede that even when "lost" traditions are rediscovered and re-evaluated in this way, reviving them in their historical forms is very difficult because of the dramatic social changes that have occurred. But the example of Edo offers a lesson transcending the changes over time that people possess an inherent wisdom for existing in harmony with nature. The spirit of thrift and aversion to waste remained alive even when Edo grew to be a large city; they persisted among the Japanese people at some level even in the recent decades of Japan's booming economic growth.

The Kenyan environmentalist Wangari Maathai found inspiration in the Japanese term *mottainai,* which describes this aversion to waste. In a meeting with me (in February 2005), Dr. Maathai said that the word *mottainai* encapsulated the spirit of reverence for nature and making the best, fullest possible use of our limited resources—an ideology that treasures rather than exploits nature. Partly because of Dr. Maathai's reappraisal of the term, the spirit of *mottainai* has in recent years undergone a re-evaluation, and the 3Rs have become well-established keywords of hands-on environmentalism.

WEIZSÄCKER: The 3R philosophy that emerged in Japan is a great concept. It essentially describes a cyclical economy instead of an extracting economy, in which all necessary resources are extracted from nature. Of course, the Japanese are also continuing to extract from nature, but still they have developed a concept of a cyclical economy, which is for the most part sustainable.

What we are most lacking in the world today is a long-term vision for the future, which could also be described as reverence for the worth and dignity of life—a phrase that I believe you use in your 2012 environment proposal. The 3R principle also mentioned there is very important, as are Dr. Maathai's activities, which are all quite constructive. These crucial ideas are very well formulated.

You mention the Edo period; of course, there is renewed interest in the lifestyle of the Edo period, but if you look at the business or political decisions being made in Japan today, they have little relation to that period. They have more to do with the Harvard Business School than with any Japanese tradition, and the same is true for Germany. So if the question is what is the biggest challenge, it's the loss of appreciation for the long-term perspective and the loss of wisdom that existed in earlier times, both in Asia and in Europe. It is lost to us now. The traditional wisdom of the Edo period is unknown to the young generation.

In Japan, momentous change occurred in the middle of the nineteenth century, an event of which all of today's Japanese are proud. The Meiji Restoration brought Japan to the vanguard of technological modernization. But it also came with many of the downsides we have been addressing.

Similarly, the Enlightenment, represented in Germany by Immanuel Kant and perhaps Wilhelm von Humboldt, while creating modern Germany, eventually became a double-edged sword. German industry soon also became a war industry, and the industrialized Kaiserreich (German empire) became an aggressive power triggering World War I. Also, in the United Kingdom, where the Enlightenment was represented by Adam Smith, the effects were both positive and negative. His praise of selfishness as a motor of wealth creation can easily be misused to legitimize selfish companies, an imperialist empire, and social Darwinism.

I feel we need a new Enlightenment, using of course the ideas of Kant, Smith, Jean-Jacques Rousseau, and others who were right, as well, of course, as those of similar thinkers in Japan, whom I admit I do not know. We need to combine what is still right and true from the Enlightenment with the necessities of the present—the imperative of sustainable, nondestructive development.

We need an alliance between Asia and Europe, I suggest, to make a new Enlightenment happen. If this dialogue between you and me can help support the necessary political dialogue, the political alliance, that would be wonderful. Japan, South Korea, and China subscribe to a sustainable use of technology, to a state that can manage and finance public goods and infrastructures, and to global rules protecting the environment. In the United States, Canada, or Brazil, I seem to observe much opposition to all global rulemaking and a basically naïve view of limitless resources that we can exploit without hesitation.

IKEDA: As you have said, philosophies and thought systems are interpreted in differing ways in differing historical and social contexts, and because of this can have both positive and negative effects. This is why it is crucial for us to seek out the true intent of a philosophy or system of ideas, always bearing in mind why it was articulated—for what purpose and in response to what conditions.

President Makiguchi, who envisioned a future era of peace and harmony, studied not only Eastern thought but the philosophies of many stimulating Western thinkers, including Kant and Rousseau. While imprisoned for his beliefs, Mr. Makiguchi made a special study of Kant's thought.

The attainment of the perpetual peace that Kant adopted as a goal, as well as the establishment of a sustainable society in which we live in harmony with the natural environment and protect the rich biodiversity of our planet, is an important challenge for us in the twenty-first century, and we must shoulder the responsibility of opening the way to making it a reality. It is also the challenge that we of the SGI, an organization of the people based on the Buddhist philosophy placing the sanctity of life as the top priority, have undertaken as our social responsibility in the 192 countries and territories where we are established. We are committed to working together with like-minded individuals and organizations around the world, expanding a network of solidarity, to accomplish this unprecedented goal and make this cherished dream of humanity a reality. I want to continue to pursue with you, Dr. Weizsäcker, a new Enlightenment to create a future of lasting peace and a sustainable society.

Social and Ecological Justice

WEIZSÄCKER: I fondly recall the enjoyable opportunity in March 2010 to participate in the Institute of Oriental Philosophy symposium on the theme "Global Environmental Problems and Ethics" and taking part in very satisfying and productive discussions with other scholars and researchers. In my keynote speech on that occasion, I noted that while science and technology can do a lot to lead to a peaceful and sustainable world, there is an additional need to effect critical changes in economics and politics.

IKEDA: It is an important point, one that should not be restricted to policy changes in a single nation but rather applied to global society.

The United Nations is focusing on what agenda should be adopted following 2015, the endpoint of the United Nations' Millennium Development Goals. In May 2013, a high-level panel at the United Nations delivered a report on the goals to be achieved by 2030, suggesting five major aims: (1) putting an end to extreme poverty; (2) taking quick action with sustainable development as its primary objective; (3) transforming economies to create

employment and inclusive growth; (4) creating peace and account-
able governance; and (5) forging a new global partnership based
on shared recognition of our mutual equality as human beings.[1]
In February 2013, prior to the UN report, the European Commission announced that the MDGs and the Sustainable Development
Goals initiated by Rio+20 in June 2012 should be tackled together
through a combined approach. Consequently, it called for efforts
such as guaranteeing a "decent life for all" the inhabitants of the
planet and managing the Earth's natural resources on a sustainable basis.[2]

In the process of examining these new goals, I believe it is
vital not only to discuss them in terms of public policy but also to
explore them from the broader perspective of human civilization.
In my 2013 peace proposal, I stressed the importance of remedying
the pathology of civilization decried by Goethe in his masterwork
Faust, where he depicts the human drive to employ any method to
fulfill one's desires by the quickest means possible with no regard
for the suffering that this may inflict upon others.[3]

It seems to me that this pathology underlies many of the threats
facing our world today. We see it in nuclear weapons, the use of
which would "defend" the nation possessing them at the price of
humanity's extinction; in a society where free market competition
is glorified at the cost of widening economic disparities and the
conscious neglect of its most vulnerable members; in the unabated
pace of ecological destruction driven by the prioritization of economic growth; and in a global food crisis brought about by commodity speculation.

I am reminded of your conclusion to *Earth Politics*, in which you
stressed the following: "We would...need a new view of civilisa-
tion and culture in the Century of the Environment."[4] My questions for you are: What are the key parameters of a new civilization
to which we should aspire in the twenty-first century? What points

in particular should we focus on in reconsidering the aims and roles of government and economics?

WEIZSÄCKER: I think there are many different factors that need reconsideration, but I would suggest in particular the importance of establishing social justice and ecological justice. You mentioned the global food crisis as one of the threats facing our world today. Taking that as an example, one of the major causes for the crisis is the waste of food resources in the West and other affluent nations such as Japan.

There are those who argue the need for the genetic engineering of foods to increase production, making the assumption that increased consumption of food demands increased production. But I believe that very assumption is in fact erroneous. Genetic engineering of food may be effective in producing more food for the rich, but that is not the answer to the larger food shortage problem.

If one's goal is to produce food for the hungry, a far more effective method is to give them land on which to grow their own food. The truth of this was already well established by Frances Moore Lappé, in her co-authored book, published in the 1970s, *Food First: Beyond the Myth of Scarcity*. Ms. Lappé was focusing on the Sahel zone, a belt south of the Sahara Desert running east and west across northern Africa that was at the time suffering terrible food shortages. In her study, she discovered the shocking fact that the countries of the Sahel zone, which were undergoing extreme famine, were actually exporting food to the United States and Europe, and the amount of their exports exceeded the amount of food they were receiving through international hunger relief.

Why did this happen? Because the impoverished residents of the Sahel zone didn't own the land. The majority of the land was owned by foreign food growers, who had no interest in producing food to feed the local people and were focused solely on growing cash crops for export.

Though the situation is different today from that described by Ms. Lappé in the 1970s, the essence of the phenomena remains unchanged. The food shortages in various parts of the world today are created by what is called *land grabbing*. In other words, foreign interests, such as investors and banks, buy up all the fertile land suitable for food production and then use it to grow crops—such as corn for ethanol for automobile fuel—that benefit their markets. The developed nations are grabbing up the farmlands of the developing nations in the pursuit of profits. This entire situation, in my opinion, is a product of market fundamentalism, which ranks profit above everything else and has no concern for social justice.

IKEDA: When considering food shortage, then, we should not focus solely on balancing supply with demand but instead reframe the question to ask why those who are in genuine need for food are denied it.

According to a study conducted in Japan, what is known as food loss—food that is edible but, because it is either unused or unsold, is discarded by households and businesses—amounts to 5–8 million tons annually in Japan.[5] The total global amount of food aid given to countries with food shortages comes to some 4 million tons. Japan alone discards more than this amount. This is the kind of situation to which you are referring when you cite the food wastage.[6] Although Japan is relatively advanced when it comes to the 3Rs, we need to remedy the current situation by reconsidering our dietary practices and resolving this problem of food wastage.

The land grabbing you refer to is also intensifying with each passing year. According to one international nongovernmental organization, foreign investors now own approximately 27 million hectares of farming land in Africa, with an estimated 10 percent of the arable land of Ethiopia and 15 percent of the arable land of Sierra Leone under foreign ownership.[7] A similar situation is spreading in Asia and Central and South America, and some have raised the alarm that this is in danger of becoming a new form of colonialism. Even if work to achieve the MDGs ameliorates food shortage, these efforts will remain little more than a stopgap unless we devote attention and action to rectify this developing trend.

In my peace proposals, I have repeatedly emphasized that the effort to achieve the MDGs must not become preoccupied merely with meeting their cited objectives; we should not forget that the highest priority should be restoring the well-being of suffering individuals. If we fixate solely on macro goals in the form of numerical targets and overlook the real-world plight of people, our priorities will have been fatally skewed.

I have also stressed that rather than looking upon threatened populations as passive recipients of aid and development assistance, it is paramount to focus on their empowerment, enabling them as protagonists to resolve their own challenges and bring their own boundless potential and strengths to fullest flower. In this regard, I agree with your view that the key is to provide land to those suffering from food shortages, so they can grow their own food.

In recent years, the idea of food sovereignty—that the people of developing nations have the right to grow the crops they want on their own land, through their own efforts—is gaining momentum. Respect for this kind of ownership is, in my opinion, a crucial factor not only with regard to the problem of food shortage but also for achieving social justice in global society.

THE TLC FACTOR

WEIZSÄCKER: I was strongly influenced in adopting the viewpoint I have just expressed by the economist Ernst Friedrich Schumacher. I knew him personally, and he was a wonderful person.

In one of his lectures, after speaking on food issues, he asked his audience, "Do you know the TLC factor?"

"What chemical is TLC?" I asked him.

"It's not a chemical," he replied. "It stands for 'tender loving care.'"

He explained that when people owned their land, they managed to produce five times as much food per acre as industrial farmers. The TLC factor that Dr. Schumacher was referring to did not register on the radars of industrial farmers, and it had not occurred to researchers in the agricultural sciences. What Dr. Schumacher pointed out made me realize that the solution to the world's food problems has less to do with markets than self-motivation, less with employing more farmers than with fostering more self-employed farmers.

IKEDA: The TLC factor emerges from a strong bond between people and nature—in this case, the soil. In his renowned 1971 work *Small Is Beautiful: A Study of Economics as if People Mattered*, Dr. Schumacher explained his views on agriculture as follows:

> A wider view sees agriculture as having to fulfill at least three tasks:
>
> —to keep man in touch with living nature, of which he is and remains a highly vulnerable part;
>
> —to humanise and ennoble man's wider habitat; and
>
> —to bring forth the foodstuffs and other materials which are needed for a becoming life.
>
> I do not believe that a civilisation which recognises only the third of these tasks, and which pursues it with such ruthlessness and violence that the other two tasks are not merely neglected but systematically counteracted, has any chance of long-term survival.[8]

Rereading this now, one can take it as both a prediction and caveat issued by Dr. Schumacher that a phenomenon similar to land grabbing would occur. His reference to the "ruthlessness and violence" with which civilization pursues its goals also resonates with the "pathology of civilization" that I noted in the context of Goethe's *Faust* in my peace proposal (2013). Without a full-fledged attempt to remedy this pathology, the creation of a genuinely sustainable society may be unattainable.[9]

Dr. Schumacher argued that this pathology is "due to the fact that, as a society, we have no firm basis of belief in any meta-economic values, and when there is no such belief the economic calculus takes over."[10] What we need now is to reexamine what the proper relationship between human beings and nature should be and what we must not neglect, either by omission or commission, in society.

The Mahayana Buddhist view of nature regards human beings and nature, human beings and the land, as inseparable. Nichiren wrote, "The living beings and their environments are not two things, and one's self and the land one inhabits are not two things."[11] In other words, all life, including human life, exists in a relationship of mutual interdependence and support, the natural environment and living beings joined by deep, indivisible bonds.

"Life is shaped by its environment,"[12] Nichiren also wrote, stressing that we must never forget to have deep gratitude for the blessings of nature and that our lives are supported by our relationships with all other living things. Our ties to nature must be based on the realization and ensuing sense of responsibility that "Without the body, no shadow can exist, and without life, no environment."[13] Or to borrow Dr. Schumacher's words to express this idea in contemporary terms, we must devote the utmost tenderness, love, and care to the environment, and, by striving to protect nature and the ecosystem, lead lives in which our humanity shines its brightest.

In this sense, I am in profound agreement with your emphasis on establishing social justice and ecological justice to create a sustainable global society.

The United Nations set the period from 2005 to 2015 as the Water for Life Decade, and the year 2013 as the International Year of Water Cooperation. I believe that social justice and ecological justice are also important factors in considering the issue of water resources.

WATER: A BASIC HUMAN RIGHT

WEIZSÄCKER: I'm not a water expert, but I believe there are four major ways in which water shortages can be ameliorated.

The first is related to the cost of water in a country and the cost of water used in agriculture in that country. The unbelievable fact is that, with the exception of the Netherlands and a few other countries, most countries set the cost of agricultural water at zero or something very close to zero. Despite that, people everywhere complain about the shortage of water. Australia and Israel use drip irrigation instead of flood irrigation. By using this water-saving method, they can produce at least three times more food per gallon (about 3.78 liters) of water. That's one important aspect. Of course, one still must make sure that farmers would not be impoverished by having to pay the actual cost of the water they use. But if they can produce three times the food per gallon of water, they shouldn't be impoverished.

The second way to maximize water resources is to purify water that has been used. This is an inescapable duty for creating sustainable urban living environments. Before reaching the North Sea, the water of the River Rhine travels through numerous cities in Switzerland, France, Germany, and the Netherlands, and tends to be used and/or recycled about ten times on its journey, which is perhaps the reason that Germany does not suffer from a water shortage, even in the low-lying North Rhine-Westphalia region. The cities of the North Rhine-Westphalia area receive Rhine water in a reasonably clean state.

Actually, to the best of my knowledge, the water leaving the North Rhine-Westphalia region is in fact cleaner than when it arrived there. Germany has amazing water purification technology—another important measure for dealing with the problem of water shortages. Unfortunately, most countries of the world do not employ such technologies. It is important for them to do so as quickly as possible.

The third way to deal with water shortages is to increase water efficiency in the private sector. In chapter 2 of *Factor Four,* we cited the example of a certain German paper manufacturer that, by the adoption of internal purification systems, managed to demonstrate a tenfold increase in water productivity in the paper-production process. This company was constantly recycling its water. It was motivated to do so by the high costs imposed on waste-water discharge. To avoid those costs, the manufacturer stored all its water inside the factory, purifying and recycling it, which increased the company's profitability. The same approach can be used in steel foundries and other industries. The efficient use of water in manufacturing is very important.

The fourth approach to dealing with water shortages is to supply more water, either by building more dams or by pumping more water from underground. Pumping more water from underground sources depletes the water table, however, and should be avoided since it is not sustainable.

IKEDA: All of the points you mention are important if we are to make the most of our precious, irreplaceable water sources and establish conditions for the sustainable use of natural resources. Water shortages, like food shortages, threaten the very survival of many people around the world.

The United Nations Development Programme Human Development Report 2006 states,

> Water, the stuff of life and a basic human right, is at the heart of a daily crisis faced by countless millions of the world's most vulnerable people—a crisis that threatens life and destroys livelihoods on a devastating scale.[14]

It warns, "Like hunger, deprivation in access to water is a silent crisis experienced by the poor and tolerated by those with the resources, the technology and the political power to end it."[15]

Improving water use was included as one of the issues within the Millennium Development Goals Report 2012, which declares that the goal of "halving the proportion of people who lack dependable access to improved sources of drinking water" was achieved ahead of the 2015 deadline. In 2015, however, more than 600 million people around the world will still be using unsafe water sources.[16]

The UN General Assembly in 2010 adopted a measure declaring access to safe, clean drinking water, as well as to sanitation, a basic human right, and growing numbers of people around the world are insisting that water should be made a public or semi-public resource. In February 2013, more than one million people in Europe signed a petition endorsing the declaration of water not as a commodity but a public good, marking the possibility that it will become the first European Citizens' Initiative in the European Union to garner the necessary support for adoption.

Speaking of "public goods," you called for their increased recognition in *Factor Five*:

> We welcome the emergence of a new, more balanced Zeitgeist. We do not want a return to the extreme counter model of the exaltation of the state and the denigration

of the market. What our world needs is market efficiency and liberation from the ideology of market fundamentalism, together with a state that is committed to the public interest and is capable of long-term action.[17]

Germany is widely known for having adopted many national policies based on this concept of public goods from the period immediately following World War II. What factors do you see as underlying this?

Ending Market Fundamentalism

WEIZSÄCKER: To discuss this, it is necessary to look into the history of the social market economy in Germany. This was adopted as a political strategy in the early years following World War II under the immense threat of the expansion of communism in Europe. The former US general and later Secretary of State George C. Marshall realized that to contain or stop communism, the West had to adopt policies that offered generous support to the poor, to prevent them from being attracted by the promises of socialism. Socialism addressed itself primarily to the poor and underprivileged, and there were many poor in Europe and worldwide at the time. The market economy had the advantage of market efficiency, which also appealed to the poor. The Marshall Plan for reviving Europe was a remarkable symbol of American generosity. Having lost more than 100,000 soldiers in the fighting in Europe, instead of taking brutal revenge on its former enemies, the United States gave them aid.

It was a brilliant move that was extremely well received by those who later came to be the majority force in the new German democracy, with close ties to the Catholic Church. Konrad Adenauer, serving as chancellor of West Germany from 1949 to

1963, was the first political leader in this country who was not a Protestant. With keen political insight, Adenauer realized the importance of overcoming the old factionalism among the conservatives and rallied his political allies to achieve that.

During the German Empire and the Weimar Republic, the Catholic-dominated German Center Party (Deutsche Zentrumspartei) and the Protestant-dominated German National People's Party (Deutschnationale Volkspartei), which both represented conservative thinking, were rivals that never really cooperated. Adenauer, although very much a Catholic, felt that his party, the Christian Democratic Union, should reflect *Christian* ethics, not solely *Catholic*. The Protestants were very happy with his political thinking. One of the manifestations of his strategy was his foreign policy and his thoroughgoing support of the Marshall Plan. Another was his social welfare policies, based on Catholic tradition, which can be traced back to Biblical times.

Jesus, who demonstrated consistent concern for the poor, would have been a socialist in modern terms. This longstanding tradition was reinvented, and it took the shape since the nineteenth century of what is called Catholic social teaching (Katholische soziallehre).[18] This tradition, though never dominant among the Church hierarchy or clergy, had a strong political influence. In a sense, you could say Adenauer, with his excellent political instincts, developed a social market economy rooted in Catholic social teaching.

There were others aside from Adenauer who made important contributions to the idea of the social market economy. Perhaps the most important was Alfred Müller-Armack, who was in a sense the father of the concept.

Essentially, the conservative idea of the social market economy was the product of a clever and instinctive opportunism of the time to confront socialism by emphasizing social welfare, as opposed to classical conservative thinking.

IKEDA: You are saying that in addition to the international situation in which postwar West Germany found itself, the emphasis by Chancellor Adenauer and other German political figures on social welfare rooted in religious traditions played a major role in the adoption of national policy.

In April 1990, after the end of the Cold War and just prior to German reunification, I met with Heinrich Barth, the chancellor's personal adviser and assistant secretary, as well as former chairman of the Konrad Adenauer Foundation (Konrad-Adenauer-Stiftung). We discussed how Chancellor Adenauer, while still the mayor of Cologne, adopted various initiatives of great public benefit in education and the environment. He was instrumental in reopening the University of Cologne, which had been closed for more than a century, and launched an initiative for the greening of the city in response to growing concerns over pollution. In June 1991, after Germany's reunification, I met Dr. Barth again in Bonn, and he expressed high hopes for your uncle's presidency.

I first met President Weizsäcker shortly after my second meeting with Dr. Barth. With a steady, serious demeanor, President Weizsäcker said that we should be concerned not just with material prosperity but with humanity itself, its solidarity and harmonious coexistence—thoughts which made a deep impression on me.[19]

He asked me about Japan and how it regarded materialism and the way in which human beings should lead their lives. I responded with my frank opinion that Japanese society is evolving at a rapid pace—the changes are coming so fiercely that the Japanese sometimes get lost and are confused as to where they stand. The majority of these changes, sadly enough, have been toward an expanding materialism. Like so many others elsewhere in the world, their lives have become dominated by these material pursuits that, in one sense, have obscured the human spirit.

When choosing a job, I explained to him, many young Japanese base their decisions on such things as whether the job pays well, whether it is easy, and whether it offers long vacations. Young people have all but forgotten the spirit of working for society's good, and a degenerate individualism has risen up in its place. To expect a tree to flourish when its deepest roots have withered does not stand to reason. Thoughtful, conscientious people are deeply concerned about Japan's future. The struggle to achieve something worthy takes a lifetime, while destruction takes but an instant. I concluded that we are battling to reverse this destructive trend, hoping to expand the bounds of spirituality, enabling it to surge throughout society like a mighty river.[20]

When President Weizsäcker visited Japan in August 1995, on the fiftieth anniversary of the end of World War II, he spoke at a large public symposium. He described the Germans and Japanese as being industrious with an economic orientation but added that while both nations follow the principles of the free market economy, they have at times gone too far. Their orientation, for example, has forced people to compete against one another from an early age, reinforcing a materialistic worldview. What we need to do, he said, is learn to think and work together from an ecological perspective and tackle the manifold challenges in building a better future while maintaining this solidarity.[21]

Germany and Japan were once militaristic societies that invaded other countries while ruthlessly engaged in thought control and xenophobic persecution of their own citizens. This led to ultranationalist absolutism and horrific results, one of the lessons of the twentieth century that we must never forget. Now, in the twenty-first century, the market fundamentalism you mentioned is in danger of becoming a new form of absolutism—a development to which we must put an end.

WEIZSÄCKER: Allowing national ideology to become an absolutism was a characteristic of communist states in the past. Such dictatorships led to corrupt regimes. It is important to recognize that when ideology takes priority over everything else, it also negatively affects the environment. When the state intervenes in the private lives and the thoughts of its citizens, it not only violates their human rights, it is also counterproductive to building a rich and strong society.

What we need is a liberal state in the European sense. "Liberal" in this sense means tolerant and forgiving. It also means an awareness of long-term public goods, investment in and maintenance of infrastructure, and state support for all other aspects of society that would not prosper under a pure market regime. For example, the market will never provide primary education and basic health care for the poor. I mentioned infrastructures—the markets won't build roads, provide sewage treatment, or law and order. The market won't create the police force we need to protect the citizenry from criminal activity or maintain judicial and legal systems. The state needs to establish and maintain these systems and receive enough revenue to do so.

At the same time, markets need to be similarly tolerant of and amenable to these services the state provides. They cannot be allowed to pursue maximum profit and ignore the adverse impact that the logic of the market, when left unchecked, has on peoples and societies. Market fundamentalism tends to lead to two very unpleasant extremes—dictatorship and loss of freedom.

REAL WEALTH

IKEDA: The global financial crisis that started in 2008, triggered by the US subprime loan debacle and the bankruptcy of Lehman Brothers, was an immense blow and cause of great turmoil to countries around the world. Behind the collapse of trust in the financial system that provoked this crisis was the explosive expansion of the highly speculative market for derivative financial products, which far exceeded the real economy in scale. When this market collapsed, the damage threatened the very foundations of the real economy. Though it cannot be denied that the pursuit of wealth has to an extent been a driving force for social progress, the lessons of this crisis, in which millions of people suddenly found themselves in desperate straits, are that we need to reexamine the real purpose of the economy and the true meaning of wealth.

Hazel Henderson, the futurist, once told me:

> The GNP (Gross National Product) is a material measure. Beyond a certain level, it's like judging adults by a growth index. What we want from adults is not more physical growth but maturity and wisdom.[22]

I find this an accessible way of explaining the issue. Just as we can't judge people's true worth only by their height, we need to look at things from multiple perspectives to determine whether they are genuinely beneficial for the people in a given society.

You have likewise observed, "Health, happiness and personal fulfillment are not of necessity closely linked to a growth in GNP or employment."[23] Instead, you urged in *Factor Five* (chapter 11) that we need more relevant measures of real wealth—like the Index for Sustainable Economic Welfare and the Human Development Index, a standardized measurement used by the United Nations Development Programme—and more discussion of the inconsistencies and incompleteness that come with the Gross Domestic Product yardstick.

WEIZSÄCKER: I believe that the term *Index for Sustainable Economic Welfare* comes from Herman Edward Daly, who used to be with the World Bank and is also a member of the Club of Rome. In his writings, he described the increasing discrepancy between the welfare of the populace and the GDP of the nation.

Another report to the Club of Rome, *Taking Nature Into Account* by Wouter van Dieren, touches upon similar themes. These and other thinkers are part of a worldwide trend to seek alternative measures to the GDP. The European Union in 2007, I believe, organized a conference in Brussels titled "Beyond GDP." The German Bundestag has created a Study Commission on Growth, Well-being, and Quality of Life. One of the questions the commission pursues is new measures of well-being.

However, the only country to actually adopt a measure of welfare other than the GDP is Bhutan, with roughly 700,000 inhabitants. They have introduced what they call a Gross National Happiness Index.

Actually, I have been asked to join a team led by Herman Daly's friend and colleague Robert Costanza, who is presently working in Australia, to help globalize the GNH Index. The team will look at what the GNH really means to the people of Bhutan and how much of that can be transferred to other economies. This is a significant effort, I believe.

IKEDA: Speaking of Bhutan, in the fall of 2011, the young king and queen of Bhutan visited the Tohoku area that had been struck by the March 2011 earthquake and tsunami, where they encouraged elementary school students and other local residents. It was a memorable gesture that remains fresh in the minds of many Japanese.

There is growing interest in Japan in Bhutan's use of GNH as a measure of its people's welfare. As you know, GNH is based on the four pillars of sustainable, equitable socioeconomic development, environmental conservation, reservation and promotion of culture, and good governance. It is measured by surveying the populace on seventy-two specific indicators based on these four pillars.[24]

Among the indicators are some interesting questions. For example:

"Do the members of your family care about each other?"
"How much do you trust your neighbors?"
"On an average how many days did you spend during the past 12 months doing voluntary activity on your own?"
"Do you plant trees around your farm or houses?"
"Rate the performance of the central government in reducing the gap between rich and poor."
"To what extent do you trust media?"[25]

Herein lies the notion that, while economic growth and social development are vital to a country and her people, such factors must be evaluated in the context of harmonious relationships with the natural environment, traditional culture, family and friends, and the community.

Buddhism serves as the foundation of traditional Bhutanese culture, and the concept behind the GNH—finding the proper balance between material and spiritual well-being—reflects, I believe, the Buddhist teaching of the Middle Way that transcends polar extremes. Considering the factors built into the GNH, one can see an underlying Buddhist spirit of mutual interdependence and support, as well as the philosophy of striving to create a community built on mutual respect.

King Ashoka of the Maurya Empire in ancient India governed his dominion with Shakyamuni's teachings. After experiencing terrible regret at the large numbers killed in his military assaults on other kingdoms, Ashoka underwent a profound change of heart and adopted various policies for his people's welfare. He provided relief to the poor, established hospitals and parks, had wells dug and roads built, and also had trees planted and encouraged the cultivation of medicinal herbs. He instituted fair, egalitarian treatment under the law and protected freedom of religion. He encouraged a life of restraint and frugality, one drawing satisfaction from modest means and resources.[26] All of these policies are based on such Buddhist principles as dependent origination, compassion, and the Middle Way. He extended these principles to protect animals and the rest of nature.

Ashoka firmly believed that the king (that is, political leaders) should rule based on Dharma—the principle of a right life—and had the duty to promote the happiness of his subjects, the people.[27] The first and foremost duty of those engaged in government should be to build a society in which people can experience happiness, rather than to establish a nation's greatness by military or economic aggrandizement. This is a principle that is surely just as important now as in Ashoka's day, different as the two periods may be.

While questions remain as to whether GNH may be applied as currently constructed to nations other than Bhutan, it will be interesting to see what conclusions Robert Costanza and your team arrive at. At the very least, my hope is that the way will open to achieve genuine social progress by incorporating the GNH index or similar indices of human happiness and dignity.

WEIZSÄCKER: Aside from the GNH used in Bhutan, Herman Daly and Wouter van Dieren, whom I mentioned earlier, as well as Manfred Max-Neef, another member of the Club of Rome, have offered brilliant ideas on this subject. Why, in spite of this, is no contemporary political leader (with the exception of Bhutan's leaders) willing to adopt any new measure of wealth? My answer to that question is clear and concrete. Employment and fiscal income are two politically very important parameters, and they are regarded by political leaders as the top priorities.

It is universally asserted that the economic troubles afflicting Greece can only be overcome with economic growth. Unemployment has reached disastrous levels in southern Europe today. In such a situation, people do not hope for happiness, they hope for economic growth and find their hope for the future in that. Generally, economic growth has high priority in situations of economic crisis.

The next question is: How can we harmonize happiness with stable public finance and steady employment? Unfortunately, those who have studied alternatives to GNP as a measure of welfare have not yet dealt with or considered this problem.

The Informal Sector

IKEDA: In the conclusion to *Earth Politics,* you speak of the need to move beyond economic policy to address these issues on both a deeper and more encompassing level from a civilizational perspective. In this context, you say that while the idea of work has been reduced in today's world to wage-earning labor, there is a need to give more recognition to such forms of self-motivated work (*eigenarbeit*) as childcare and social activities:

> Finally, and above all, even now the formal economy based on employment would be totally helpless if the "informal sector" did not still exist. Sleeping, eating, loving and bringing up children are not subordinate activities we could do without but the indispensable foundation of all human existence. Economic theory has a shocking tendency to repress this simple fact.[28]

You go on to say that the "formal and informal economy ought once again to be on a par with each other,"[29] which would represent a major step toward a new model of wealth. What are your thoughts on the world situation today with regard to the informal economy?

WEIZSÄCKER: My observation is that this informal economy is actually stronger in poor countries and in the United States than it is in Germany. The reasons for this in poor countries are simple. If people are impoverished, if they have very little money, the better survival strategy is to do some gardening and cooking of their own instead of waiting on money to buy things or services.

Yet, politicians of developing countries in general, and many among those running the international agencies and organizations promoting development, see it as a goal to sever the attachment to the informal economy that citizens of poor countries have. This assumption is made because, historically, overcoming the informal sector has been the road to prosperity, under the imperative of the division of labor, as in Europe, Japan, and other countries.

The most extreme form of this has manifested itself as Taylorism, or scientific management. In a less extreme form, it is the division of labor as articulated by Adam Smith—it is good for the baker to make more bread than he can consume, because in so doing, he frees others from the need to bake bread, and they can turn their energies to other occupations, such as being barbers, farmers, and other professionals. The insight has been credited since the eighteenth century with bringing prosperity to many countries and is likewise regarded as indispensable for placing developing countries on the path to economic growth. This economic model, however, must be recognized as inherently antagonistic to the informal sector.

Since the informal sector of the economy has been regarded as being antithetical to genuine economic development, one cannot talk realistically about a revival of the informal sector without knowing why it was destroyed.

In the United States, the situation is different from developing countries. There, you have a very weak state. Therefore, there is a substantial loss of public goods, which, as you will remember, markets never produce. In this situation, where some people amass great wealth, their sense of personal responsibility leads them to do unpaid civil work for their community, church, and all kinds of other venues and causes, substituting for the public sector, which would shoulder those functions in Germany or in Japan, where the public sector still works.

These two situations—the informal sector of developing countries and that of the United States—need to be distinguished from each other. The developing countries' situation is a little bit more like Germany in the eighteenth century and the American situation where the state was in a very good situation in the days of Thomas Jefferson, Abraham Lincoln, or Franklin D. Roosevelt. But after Jimmy Carter, with the advent of Ronald Reagan, the state was deliberately weakened; that was Reagan's credo.

Today, the United States needs all those unpaid services, because the state can no longer provide them. Still, I believe what we wrote in *Earth Politics*: In order to reestablish prosperity outside the economic measurement of GNP and GDP, the informal sector is necessary.

IKEDA: The key to grasping the importance of the economy's informal sector, as I see it, is the concept of self-motivated work of which you spoke earlier. It is utterly disassociated from any self-interest; remuneration is not a consideration; it is the kind of labor you alone choose and evaluate. In addition to being "work that belongs to you, that you mostly shape yourself, and that may also shape you," it is also work that is "done for your family or for yourself, for your neighbors, and for future generations."[30]

While work for wages—paid labor—may alienate us from our humanity or demean our dignity and sense of personal worth, self-motivated work, though in most cases unpaid, is a source of self-worth and self-validation and gives us fulfillment in having helped our family members and others in our lives. It seems to me that the initiative informing such self-motivated work is consonant with a life lived in accord with the Buddhist spirit of compassion. The Buddhist concept of compassion contains two aspects: the desire to share joy with others, to bring about their well-being and happiness *(maitrī)*, and the desire to embrace the suffering of others as one's own and ameliorate their anguish *(karunā)*. *Maitrī*, moreover, derives from the word *mitra,* or friend.

In describing the importance of compassion, Shakyamuni employed the simile of a mother's feelings—the very epitome of self-motivated work: "Just as a mother would protect her only child at the risk of her own life, even so, let him cultivate a boundless heart towards all beings."[31] Nichiren also said, "'Joy' means that oneself and others together experience joy,"[32] and, "Both oneself and others together will take joy in their possession of wisdom and compassion."[33] Thus, the joy that emerges from the innermost depths of our lives when we act not merely for ourselves but for the sake of others is the greatest of all joys.

I feel that this joy in life and the ties between human beings as they share one another's sufferings and travails is greatly diminished in society today. In countering this trend, you mention in *Factor Four* a "snug harbour for children in their time of growing up and exploring the world"[34] as one important aspect of the informal sector. You underscore the need to reaffirm the significance of the informal sector as a place in which people know one another very well (which cannot be measured by market value) and shape their communal society with a shared commitment.

Then, you go on to describe the informal sector as a safe haven that includes not only the family but our neighborhoods, schools, local shops of our towns, our educational and religious institutions, our recreational clubs, and all our other social gatherings. I am struck by this description, for I feel it could also be applied to the SGI. As a Buddhist lay organization, the SGI is engaged in promoting strong, warm, and supportive human relations among individuals of all races and ethnic groups, ages, and professions in countries and communities around the world.

I believe self-motivated work not only elevates people's self-worth but also plays an increasingly crucial role in reinforcing human relationships. Your wife, Christine von Weizsäcker, is the one who identified this idea of self-motivated work.

WEIZSÄCKER: Yes, she created the term *Eigenarbeit* in 1968 or so, quite early in the discussion. In the later 1970s, when we were living in Kassel, Hessen, we became friends with Ivan Illich. He was fascinated by the term because his lifelong theme was the alienation of people by their professional imperatives. In his book *Deschooling Society,* he argued that people don't only learn from schools, they learn by themselves in families, in rings of friendship. They also learn something at school, but schools do not have a monopoly on learning. For him, Eigenarbeit was an exciting, emancipatory term of the late 1970s, but unfortunately it did not have the transformative effect he had hoped for.

The trend of professionalization continues unabated. The main reason is that people want jobs, and classical jobs are disappearing, so new jobs are created by professionalizing functions that, in earlier times, were done inside the family. A case in point is pre-kindergarten daycare centers with professional nurses and teachers. They did not exist when I was a three-year-old child, and nobody cared, but now it is regarded as essential.

Billions of dollars and euros are being spent to create jobs for men and women. It is always the imperative of creating jobs that holds back Eigenarbeit. Professionalization and Eigenarbeit are antagonistic. In a sense, under today's employment conditions, professional daycare centers are a blessing for women, allowing them to work.

Reimagining Work

Ikeda: Illich's book *Shadow Work,* in which he discussed the many kinds of work that are indispensable to daily life but are performed without pay, such as housework and childcare, was published in 1981. He became friends with you and your wife prior to that, which I find intriguing.

In an interview conducted later in life, Illich reflected on those times, "Work was increasingly identified with *paid* work, and all other work was considered some kind of toil which could be identified through only one characteristic: that it was *not* paid, or not properly paid."[35] In the same interview, he added, "In a commodity-intensive society the human labor put into a use value is split up, one part is unpaid, the other paid, and it's the unpaid part which creates the possibility of paying wages."[36]

I can't help but feel that this seemingly inexorable trend of contemporary society is narrowing and distorting the true meaning of human labor. The spiritual nature of humanity is in fact mired in the process of devolving.

Dr. Schumacher, whom we mentioned earlier, is known for his keen observations on the root of the illness afflicting modern industrial society. In our effort to envision a sustainable economy based on respect for the worth and dignity of humanity, I think we need to heed once again his message in *Small Is Beautiful:*

> If it cannot get beyond its vast abstractions, the national income, the rate of growth, capital/output ratio, input output analysis, labour mobility, capital accumulation; if it cannot get beyond all this and make contact with the human realities of poverty, frustration, alienation, despair, breakdown, crime, escapism, stress, congestion, ugliness, and spiritual death, then let us scrap economics and start

afresh. Are there not indeed enough "signs of the times" to indicate that a new start is needed?[37]

WEIZSÄCKER: The words of Dr. Schumacher that you have just cited are very similar to our analysis of the problem in *Factor Four*. There, we warned:

> The time may have come to recognise what was lost with the erosion of the informal sector. . . . The modern ills of loneliness, unrest, vandalism, drug addiction and related crime may have much to do with the decline of the informal sector.[38]

The still prevailing belief among the political leadership in all societies in the world is the need to create employment. In Germany and many other nations, the idea that job creation is an issue of the highest priority has become the deeply entrenched political consensus. This situation persists in spite of the many sacrifices it demands. It will take another fifty years, I fear, before the political establishment begins to awaken to the reality of how much is being sacrificed on the altar of job creation.

In chapter 11 of *Factor Five*, we addressed this problem to a modest degree by offering a compromise. We suggested designing a society in which unemployment is overcome not by an unchecked economic growth but by sharing jobs. This actually is an idea that my wife proposed in discussions with Illich in the 1970s. She said, "Why not give all people, from infants to ninety-year-olds, women and men alike, the same identical permit to work in quantitative increments?"

A little calculation will illustrate this idea. Let us say that in Germany, with 80 million people, there are 40 million jobs—half as many jobs as people. In reality there are fewer jobs, but we'll adopt this formula to simplify the math. One job would be defined

as forty working hours per week and some holidays. Then, by definition, everybody's entitlement would be twenty hours per week,
from infants to the elderly.

Infants don't work, of course. But this model incorporates a system in which every person is provided the right to buy or sell his
or her work entitlement on the labor market. Parents can mon-
etize their child's entitlement to help out the family budget, for
example. Conversely, children can do the same when caring for
their elderly parents, exchanging the latter's entitlement of labor
into cash. Another permutation of this is that parents could halve
their workloads to care for an infant, while children could do the
same to care for their parents.

In such a society, there would be no lack of employment for anyone who wanted to work, no desperate unemployment. Everybody
would have her or his entitlement and could use it.

This concept of job-sharing, to which we allude in chapter 11
of *Factor Five*, was inspired by *Travailler Deux Heures Par Jour* (To
Work Two Hours Per Day), a book published in France in the
1970s. Two hours a day is about ten hours a week—only half of
twenty hours per week—but the authors calculated that ten hours
is sufficient for survival.

Of course, this model of job-sharing seems completely utopian
from the perspective of contemporary society. Our aim in present-
ing it was to stress the need to overcome the fear of unemployment
that is threatening all other values, including the value of family, of
freedom, as well as religious values. To change society, we strongly
emphasized the need to triumph over the fear of unemployment.

IKEDA: You raise some fascinating questions. In connection with
the issue of labor, I want to discuss the *raison d'etre* of individuals
in a graying society. Given our rapidly aging population today, it
is time to examine with even greater urgency what makes for a
better, more fulfilling life. At the same time, society as a whole

needs to take steps to make it possible for the elderly to engage in purposeful work and remain active in the world around them.

I am reminded of something that Arnold J. Toynbee told me. He said that even past eighty, he was still tackling the daily challenges of his research based on his favorite motto, *Laboremus*, Latin for "Let us get to work." Inspired by Dr. Toynbee's example, I also spend my days writing and encouraging our SGI members around the world.

Though you're in your seventies, Dr. Weizsäcker, you continue to be vigorous and in high spirits, with the world as your stage. What kind of society do you think we should build to enable the elderly to shine with a sense of purpose and self-worth, and lead fully satisfying lives?

WEIZSÄCKER: The next important step in Germany and Japan is to encourage people to work longer. This means to create jobs and part-time jobs that are particularly suited for the elderly.

There are two different aspects to this issue. One is the mathematical problem of providing social security for the elderly. Let's say that in Germany we stop working, on the average, at age sixty-three. But demographers say that our life span is expanding by about one month per year. That means that pensions that we can draw from will be diminished by one-twelfth every year, resulting in the impoverishment of the elderly. Mathematically speaking, it is clear that we simply have to work longer.

When a social security pension system for the elderly was first introduced in Germany, in the days of Otto von Bismarck, the time span between entry into the pension system and death used to be about five years. Today it is something like twenty years, or four times as long.

One answer to this problem is represented by the question that you and Dr. Toynbee, as well as many others, raise: "Why should we stop working because we are old? As long as we have the capacity to work, why shouldn't we?" The trade unions, however, are highly critical of this idea. According to them, the number of jobs or amount of work is a zero-sum game: The longer an individual works, the more unemployment that individual creates among the young. I think this is wrong, however. It is not a zero-sum game.

Actually, a little anecdote may illustrate what I'm saying. When I began working as the dean, the chief executive officer, of the Bren School of Environmental Science and Management at the University of California in Santa Barbara, I was sixty-six. I would ask my colleagues at the University of California why no one asked how old I was. The reason no one could ask my age, they explained, is because in a work context it could be regarded as ageist.

When I asked whether I was taking away some younger American's job, the response was: "That is a typically German question. We do not think that way in America. According to our way of thinking, if you do the job properly, you will be creating new jobs for ten young Americans a year." And that is what in fact I did. During my tenure of three years there, the school gained some $20 million in endowments and well-funded scientific projects. Based on interest rates, that amount could finance the employment of about thirty people.

In my present situation, I am actually paying more income taxes than I am receiving from my pensions. This means that in purely financial terms, my present work is good for the state. I'm not a liability; I am an asset to the state.

The other aspect is that in addition to the division of labor by profession that currently exists, we need a division of labor based on age as well. This has yet to be developed. With regard to the pension system, my answer is twofold: We need to provide gainful employment for the elderly so that added value is created to avoid the impoverishment of either the elderly or the young.

The young are being impoverished by excessive taxation, a substantial portion of it supporting the social security pension system and the non-working elderly. To lower taxes, we need to actively create jobs appropriate for the elderly, with appropriate remuneration and more freedom in hours.

I'm very happy now that I don't have to leave my home at 8:00 and be at my office in the morning. I can get up when I want, and still I work more than most people do in their forties. This freedom to create one's own schedule is a high value, and satisfaction is high. Doing things that I can do better than the young is also a good thing.

IKEDA: Your record of achievement is as remarkable as it is admirable. You have served as an educator, have made meaningful contributions to solving global environmental problems, and still shoulder numerous important responsibilities.

Your suggestions for our graying society are certainly noteworthy and thought-provoking. I believe it is imperative for every society to create an environment in which the elderly can work with purpose and satisfaction and lead lives of enduring hope. I believe there is no greater joy and fulfillment in life than to continue to participate in society and contribute in some way to the happiness of others and the world, no matter how old one is.

Dr. Toynbee said: "We must all become participants, whatever our degree of ability, because man is a social animal. We cannot change that."[39] Of course, working is not the only means of social involvement. I have seen many individuals who, after retiring from their jobs and resolving to spend the rest of their lives with the same passion and commitment they had in their youth, strive for the betterment of their communities, societies, and the world in general.

When one aspires to lead a truly fulfilling life, I think the freedom to create one's own schedule that you mentioned is vital. Having time to spare is not the same as freedom, and lacking spare time is not necessarily a restriction.

What matters is the will to better oneself. True freedom, I believe, shines through that unceasing process of self-development. In this sense, no life is happier than one in which people can spend their final years continuing to improve and elevate themselves, devoting their time to a great, meaningful purpose.

Dr. Toynbee said that one remains young as long as one remains interested in what will happen in the future.[40] I pledge to continue working with the utmost vigor to create a path toward a global society of peace and harmonious coexistence for the generations of young people to follow, making each and every day count to the fullest.

CONVERSATION EIGHT

Our Sustainable Future

IKEDA: In recent years, a series of abnormal weather events has caused serious damage worldwide. In a study it released in July 2013, the World Meteorological Organization reported, "The world experienced unprecedented high-impact climate extremes during the 2001–2010 decade."[1] The report cited such meteorological extremes as Hurricane Katrina, which hit the United States in 2005, the 2010 floods in Pakistan, and long-term droughts in the Amazon basin, noting that during the ten years from 2001 to 2010, more than 370,000 people died as a result of abnormal climate conditions.[2]

In 2013, typhoons of record ferocity devastated large areas of the Philippines and Vietnam, while heavy rains produced flooding in India and Canada, and many regions of the northern hemisphere experienced record heat waves. In Europe, torrential rains caused major rivers and their tributaries to overflow. The flooding in Germany, the Czech Republic, Austria, Hungary, and Slovakia received extensive media coverage in Japan.

I quickly sent messages of condolences to the stricken countries and the SGI members who live there. Japan was struck by torrential rains as well, and preparing for not only earthquakes and tsunamis but also such extreme weather events became an urgent issue for countries around the world. Have the 2013 floods raised awareness of extreme weather in Germany?

Weizsäcker: First, please allow me to express my sincere thanks for your concern about the flooding in Germany. The extreme weather events taking place around the world are also a source of great concern to me. The heavy rains and flooding in India and Canada were indeed disastrous, and one cannot help but be astonished at the horrific damage inflicted by the typhoons that struck the Philippines and Vietnam.

Though by comparison the flooding in Germany claimed far fewer lives and caused much less damage, the Danube River overflowed its banks, flooding hundreds of square miles. The worst affected were the Elbe River and its tributaries. For example, the railway bridge between Hanover and Berlin was destabilized, and it took a half-year to reopen it. Since the nineteenth century, we in Germany have built right up to our rivers' banks, but it is now becoming clear that that was a mistake.

During the last ten years, opinion has gradually come to prevail that it is better to leave open space around our rivers to reduce the damage even when large areas adjacent to rivers are flooded. The German government has taken safety measures at the local level for dealing with floods and water damage, but as weather changes create more extreme conditions, the government is increasingly aware of the threat, and public perception of imminent dangers is also growing.

Ikeda: The growing awareness of the need to reserve open space around rivers to prevent water damage is a noteworthy development. Interest in the concept of resilience in disaster prevention and relief has been growing, which I believe is a significant step forward. As you know, the idea of resilience in this context is based on the recognition that natural disasters and extreme weather can occur at any time or place, and that steps must be taken to reinforce society's ability to resist such conditions, thereby limiting or containing the resulting damage. Resilience further underscores the need to strengthen the capacity of society to recover after such disasters or extreme conditions strike.

As the floods that beset Europe in 2013 and the super typhoons that hit the Philippines and Vietnam all show, extreme weather conditions are not problems limited to a single nation but affect entire regions. With this in mind, in the peace proposal that I issued in January 2014, I called for the establishment of cooperative mechanisms at the regional level—for example, in Africa and Asia—to reduce the damage wrought by extreme weather. I also urged this resilience be reinforced in parallel with the measures being developed on a global scale by the United Nations Framework Convention on Climate Change. At the nineteenth session of the Conference of the Parties to the UNFCCC in November 2013, an agreement called the Warsaw International Mechanism for Loss and Damage—these two major themes, loss and damage associated with climate change, were discussed—was adopted.

But such response strategies remain insufficient, and I believe we must continue to devise numerous additional mechanisms. The same can be said regarding steps to counter global warming, an area in which negotiations appear to be stalled.

Germany announced at the beginning of 2014 that it had achieved the target for greenhouse gas reduction that it agreed upon in the Kyoto Protocol. We cannot but hope that other nations will follow Germany's example and be as engaged in doing the same.

RISING WATER LEVELS

WEIZSÄCKER: In the Kyoto Protocol, Germany committed itself to an average greenhouse gas emission reduction of 21 percent for the period from 2008 to 2012, compared to the base level of the year 1990. In fact, the country achieved a reduction of 23.6 percent, exceeding its target.[3] On the other hand, numerous individuals persist in spreading the fairytale that global warming has stopped over the past fifteen years.

In some sense, that is correct. Certain areas have not experienced additional warming during the last fifteen years. But many others have. In particular, the water of the oceans has warmed very, very significantly, especially around and under the Greenland ice, creating an increasingly dangerous situation. In several places, the ice has broken off in a catastrophic fashion or, at the very least, is starting to do so. Newspapers are reporting that the melting of the permafrost has also led to major coastal changes, particularly in east Siberia. With these changes, travel by ships is now possible along the northern coast of Eurasia and North America, thereby opening new avenues for excavating more coal, oil, and gas—making things worse, of course.

IKEDA: As of July 2012, as you say, 97 percent of the Greenland ice sheet revealed surface melting,[4] and its underside melting is also accelerating. The thawing of the sheet is an ongoing threat, and additional international monitoring of the process is needed.

In the lectures you gave throughout Japan, you frequently discussed the melting of the Greenland ice sheet and the accompanying rise of sea levels. Noting that many of the leading cities of Japan and Asia are at or near sea level and situated along coastlines, you stressed the dangers that rising sea levels present to the Japanese.

WEIZSÄCKER: Many years ago, I was reading an article by Michael Tooley, a British paleogeologist, in the British science magazine *Nature* (November 1989) about the significance of changes in sea levels. According to that article, sea level changes can be traced over the last 20,000 years or so, and in a period from about 7,800 years to 7,700 years ago, an enormous change occurred in a non-linear fashion—a stunning and alarming message indeed. In that hundred-year period, sea levels rose twenty-three feet. Though we can date the sea level rise to that particular century, the actual change could have occurred in a decade or even a single year within that larger time frame. The author attributed this nonlinear event to the catastrophic breaking off of the two- to three-thousand meters thick ice cap that stretched from the Hudson Bay over the Labrador Sea to Greenland.

This indicates that if ocean temperatures around and below the Greenland ice are getting warmer, the danger is indeed increasing for the ice to break off—not to melt, but to break off—causing a sea level rise of perhaps another twenty to twenty-three feet. And if the same happens with the west Antarctic ice plate, sea levels could rise 46 feet, meaning that much of Tokyo, Nagoya, Osaka, Hamburg, Amsterdam, Alexandria, Bangkok, Calcutta, and Mumbai would be under water. The same would happen to all the major Chinese seaports, as well as Manila, Jakarta, and coastal cities in the United States—New Orleans, Los Angeles, New York, and Boston.

These cities could be submerged much too quickly to build any sort of protective dams. Even if there were time, it is quite a challenge to build dams 46 feet high. That's why I believe that the real danger, probably after the end of this century, could be a nonlinear rise of sea levels. In the face of this very real possibility, we cannot afford to relax our vigilance.

IKEDA: You are reminding us that we must not forget the sudden rise in sea levels that followed the sundering of a massive chunk of glacial ice in northeastern Canada.[5] A rise in sea levels of just a few centimeters can have dire effects. As a UN report put it, "A half-meter sea level rise by 2050 would flood almost a million square kilometers—an area the size of France and Italy combined—and affect some 170 million people." The report goes on to note, "The impact will be largest in East Asia and the Pacific, where more than 63 million people are likely to be affected."[6]

Though it will be difficult to avoid such natural causes of rising sea levels as sundered ice caps, it is vital for nations to cooperate to the maximum extent possible in addressing man-made causes. Earlier, you noted that the melting of the permafrost would open "new avenues for excavating more coal, oil, and gas—making things worse. . . ." This has serious ramifications that we cannot afford to overlook.

REDISCOVERING FRUGALITY

IKEDA: In our dialogue, we have agreed upon the need to abandon the present model of a society bent on the voracious consumption of resources and establish in its place a sustainable society. In this context, I strongly agree with your advocacy in *Factor Five*, in which you cite both the importance of every individual deriving a sense of spiritual fulfillment and scientific and technological initiatives as the keys to successfully freeing ourselves from a resource-wasting society. You state that we are now entering a time in which people are rediscovering the virtues of frugality, a culture and mindset of being content with what we possess that our forebears had recognized and appreciated. Furthermore, you suggest that "frugality" may be understood in our day as "sufficiency based on efficiency." The real challenge for those in public office, in your view, is to convince their fellow citizens of the value of frugality and incorporate it into the economy and government.

You also advocate that rather than viewing this path as a "poor lifestyle," we should take pride in embracing such a sustainable way of life. I find this belief, which expresses a new vision for a sustainable society, indicative of the depths of insight that you and your *Factor Five* co-authors offer. We could thus say that a lifestyle of living in appreciation of what one already has not only helps to expand the ethos of frugality in society, it also encourages people to ennoble their lives spiritually and inspires a deep sense of personal fulfillment.

WEIZSÄCKER: In answering the question of how we can respond to the threats we face on a global scale, I have offered the ideas of efficiency and, as you have just said, sufficiency. To restate, by *efficiency*, I mean the fivefold increase of productivity, and by *sufficiency*, I mean agreeing not to use more energy, water, and minerals, and feeling satisfied and happy about that.

I freely acknowledge that frugality and sufficiency are closely connected to the wisdom of religion. A vast majority of religions of the world naturally have, as a central value, simplicity and frugality. In a certain sense, one could say that the movement away from a religious to a secular ethos has led to the abandonment of the values of frugality and sufficiency.

IKEDA: I believe that we are entering an age when religion will be called upon to play a greater role in establishing such values as frugality and sufficiency in society. However, in the promotion of these values, if people come to regard frugality, for example, as something negative, as a lifestyle that is forced upon them, as has often been the case, it will be difficult to win public endorsement of such values and expand this wave of social transformation. For the majority of people to feel personally motivated in making this lifestyle change and adhering to it, I think that it is imperative, as you note, for our notion of sufficiency to be underpinned by the sense of pride we can feel in doing what is right.

The reason that energy conservation efforts have received such wide, positive acceptance in Japan is that people believe their actions do not disadvantage anyone and are the right thing to do. Can you think of any other examples of successful social movements or changes that have been motivated by such pride and this sense of sufficiency?

Weizsäcker: I think the Transition Towns movement founded by Rob Hopkins, an environmental activist in Ireland, is an example.

To the best of my knowledge, there are numerous transition towns in existence in the world, mostly in English-speaking countries but also in Germany. The residents in such towns do not depend on goods received from outside sources and, while they lead relatively simple lives, they have chosen to focus on social interaction within the community.

The number of towns in Germany engaging in this social experiment is on the increase. The city of Freiburg is a good example. After the end of the Cold War, when French troops left the Vauban Barracks outside the city, Freiburg decided to transform a large area occupied by the former barracks into a new town section, which they named Vauban. Four out of five families in Vauban, I am told, don't own a car—not because they can't afford one, but because they find car ownership the wrong answer to the need for personal mobility. Their point of view is that they have a convenient tram running every three to five minutes, they have bicycles, and they have access to car sharing in cases where they really need a car. In this way, a new quality of life has emerged in Vauban, a lifestyle with few cars.

Vauban is recognized as a German urban area with a high level of personal happiness and a relatively large number of children, because families with children find it particularly agreeable to live in the Vauban. The fact that there are no car accidents is important in their quality of life. Vauban stands as an example of the possibility of living without energy imports, eating locally grown foods, wearing locally produced clothing, and residing in locally constructed buildings.

I believe that the residents of such communities are leading active social lives based on the principle of mutual assistance. Aware of their personal responsibilities, considerate of the community's children and their neighbors, they are striving to build sound human relations.

RECYCLING OF RESOURCES

IKEDA: It is an excellent example of a sustainable lifestyle in which one can take pride and a wonderful case study of one of the world's first eco-towns or eco-cities. My understanding is that the Transition Towns movement aims to move away from dependence on oil in order to achieve a new, sustainable society. In practical terms, it calls for community residents to work together to reduce energy consumption and to promote usage of local resources.

I'm told that an SGI member in the United Kingdom has been involved in this movement, working to enhance greater environmental awareness among children and citizens. The point that I find particularly wonderful regarding this movement is that individuals are sharing a worthy cause with their neighbors where they live now and are voluntarily engaged in such activities.

As I mentioned before, the SGI, which shares the same awareness of the problem, has developed exhibitions such as *Seeds of Change: Earth Charter and Human Potential* and *Seeds of Hope: Visions of Sustainability, Steps toward Change*, which have been shown around the world. The exhibitions encourage each individual to embrace environmental issues as a personal challenge and to take action in which each can take pride for the future's sake.

In addition, from 2011, we have sponsored *The Earth and I*, an environmental exhibition held throughout Japan to raise consciousness at the grassroots level. One section of this exhibition features environmentally friendly cities of the world that have achieved positive results through the cooperative efforts of government, business, and residents. Freiburg is introduced as a remarkable city that rid itself of privately owned automobiles through a municipal Environmental Card program (replaced with the Regio-Card in 1991).[7]

To reexamine our behavior and culture as consumers and rediscover the true value of happiness in the process of this reexamination; to find fulfillment in working with our neighbors to tackle environmental issues and drawing upon it to better our lives; and for this sense of fulfillment to serve as a foundation for the continuity of our civic action—these are the driving forces that will enable us to make the transition from a resource-wasting society to a resource-recycling society.

WEIZSÄCKER: In our society today, people are submerged in the ideology of the market and are living amid an overflowing mass of goods. In that lifestyle, one is easily fooled into thinking that sitting in front of your computer online is a substitute for actually interacting with and caring for other people.

But that is clearly wrong. What we need to create is a civilization in which a self-centered life is recognized as unacceptable and unethical, and in which caring for one's neighbors and family members is recognized as good and right.

In my home, three generations are living together, enjoying pleasant and satisfying human relations. One of our daughters and her husband, as well as their three children, are all living together under the same roof with my wife and me. We are delighted to have our grandchildren close by, and they also seem very happy to have their grandparents around. Of course, the same is true of the middle generation, my daughter and her husband. I hope that my grandchildren will experience the same good fortune that I have had in my life. What I mean to say is that from my personal experience, family relationships are an important source of happiness and satisfaction.

IKEDA: I also regard family ties as a foundation for building a lifestyle filled with satisfaction. What you've just said reminds me of a point you make in *Factor Five* that, in striving to put the principle of sustainability into action in our lives, the question we should ask ourselves is whether we can justify our behavior as consumers to our children and grandchildren. This, I believe, is an extremely important guideline for us all.

I say this because, while our concern for future generations may be genuine, it is only by relying on such tangible, specific motivational measures as our heartfelt concern for our families that we can reinforce and regulate our every action and behavior on a daily basis.

Are there any other areas that you want to emphasize from the perspective of family?

WOMEN POWER

WEIZSÄCKER: One of my best friends is from India, former president of the Club of Rome Ashok Khosla. Through his company, Development Alternatives, he has created roughly three million jobs in rural India, which is a huge achievement. At one point, he looked at the happiness and the attitudes of the people who were affected by the programs of Development Alternatives. One of the most striking things he learned is that women who found a modest job through Development Alternatives—for instance, in paper manufacturing at the village level—were actually happier. Another interesting fact he discovered was that, compared to women who lived in impoverished communities with high birthrates, women with jobs were very, very happy with only one or two children. In other words, the social security that women obtain through their jobs can make them feel happier and lead to stabilizing the population.

In the developed nations, however, happiness can be increased by *reducing* the amount of time that parents work, allowing them more time for their children. Social security systems could also be restructured so that parents agreeing on a reduction of work time in exchange for more time with their children will not suffer any losses in their social security pension.

IKEDA: Improving working conditions and ensuring social security for women and mothers is a significant issue for many nations.

I exchanged opinions on this subject with Mankombu S. Swaminathan, the Indian agricultural scientist known for his contributions to the "ever-green revolution," which saved Asia from famine. We spoke of alternative development methods to cope with poverty, carried out not by governments but by local communities, methods that are becoming widely accepted around the world.

Speaking of the need for popular reform movements, Dr. Swaminathan urged:

> The challenge today is to carry the benefits of individual experiments or individual development models to more and more people—to women, the poor and the socially and economically underprivileged. There are many affirmative sparks—the task at hand is to unite them into a great flame to illumine the whole world.[8]

If women are allowed to fully demonstrate their strengths, their contributions to social change will be immeasurable. When women are truly content with the quality of their lives and cast the light of joy upon their families, communities, and all of society, the seeds of happiness are sure to flower majestically everywhere.

Avoiding the Rebound Effect

Ikeda: While stressing the need to develop technologies that will make our use of resources more efficient, you also point out the importance of avoiding the "rebound effect"—having all efficiency gains outstripped by a rise in consumption, as has always happened in the past. You make a pointed observation, and I heartily concur with it.

To avoid the rebound effect, it is vital for people to be aware of the proper justification for enhancing resource efficiency. To win social acceptance for this effort, I believe we need to promote the underlying thinking behind it, rooting in each individual such perspectives that enrich the overall quality of our lives.

This is crucial because human greed tends to expand without limit. The Buddhist philosophy of life refers to this limitless desire on numerous occasions. For example, "Even a shower of gold cannot quench the passions."[9] Another Buddhist text states, "And were the mountain all of shimmering gold, / Not e'en twice reckoned would it be enough / For one man's wants."[10] Another Buddhist scripture warns against the way that the desires we assume we have controlled can intensify before we are aware, eventually consuming us: "He who desires different sense objects . . . , passions will overpower him, dangers will crush him and pain will follow him as water leaks into a wrecked ship."[11]

This may accurately describe the reality of the human condition today. And these insatiable human desires, enabled by the advances in modern science and technology, compel us to waste our natural resources and destroy the environment.

WEIZSÄCKER: The rebound effect, or Jevons paradox, is an empirical phenomenon that has been observed during the last 150 years, in which efficiency creates added demand—typically at lower prices for goods and services and commodities. A part of my answer to the challenge of the rebound effect is to reverse this trend by making energy, mineral resources, and water more expensive.

In order to avoid social disruption, this should be done in a ping-pong fashion—following an increase in energy productivity by an increase in energy prices, following an increase in mineral or water productivity by an increase in resource costs—with the end result that the amount you pay on average for your energy, mineral, and water remains the same each year. That, I believe, would make this shift tolerable.

Overcoming greed, to prevent a reoccurrence of the rebound

effect, requires us to explore deeply such anthropological questions as how we live our lives, what we can do, what we can desire, and how we can overcome short-term, selfish attitudes. These, of course, are the questions asked by all religions of the world, questions that are perhaps more pronounced in Buddhism than in many other religions.

IKEDA: Regarding overcoming desire, Mahayana Buddhism teaches that kindling the fires of earthly desires draws forth the "wisdom fire" of enlightenment.[12] This represents a way of life in which our desires do not consume us, but rather we control, harness, and sublimate them for a greater, higher purpose. Instead of seeking to extirpate desires, it is a process of substantive transformation through which we employ the fundamental energy of life—the yearning to improve one's circumstances, the fount of all desires—into a means to secure not simply personal gain but the happiness of self and others alike. It is from this perspective that we seek to contribute to the resolution of the problems facing modern civilization.

Again, Mahayana Buddhism teaches the bodhisattva ideal. Bodhisattvas are those who, rather than distancing themselves from the real world and its maelstrom of self-interest and earthly desires, leap right into the midst of it and—without allowing themselves to be swept away by ego or desire—embrace from the very depths of their lives the vow to act for the welfare of others and society. SGI members seek to stay true to such a way of life as we strive to uphold our Buddhist faith, and we have consistently engaged in the effort to resolve society's manifold issues in the communities in which we live and work based on our belief in life's inherent worth and dignity.

I am reminded of Aurelio Peccei's life. As you know, Dr. Peccei spent half of his life as a successful businessman before establishing the Club of Rome. He reflected that he had lived a stimulating, rewarding life, not only managing a non-profit company supporting developing nations for twenty years but being called upon to apply his skills to revive an ailing enterprise under daunting circumstances. But in circumscribing the globe again and again—crossing the equator more than 300 times—he experienced a feeling quite separate from the fulfillment he found in his work.

As he once wrote:

> I was convinced that to reclaim a piece of desert or to build a factory here and a dam there and to develop local and national plans are indispensable activities; but I also gradually realized that to concentrate practically all efforts on such individual projects or programmes, while the larger context in which they are embedded—namely, the global world condition—is steadily deteriorating, would risk becoming an exercise in futility.[13]

These thoughts and feelings culminated in his establishment of the Club of Rome. Through *The Limits to Growth* and numerous other reports, he built the foundations for the activities of the renowned think tank, which brought to the foreground concerns over the future of humanity. This dramatic shift in Dr. Peccei's mind—a narrative that began as a fundamental question on the meaning and purpose of the pursuit of what *can* be done and ended instead in the pursuit of what *ought to* be done—shows us the way to build a sustainable society.

In other words, the goal must be to expand outward the bounds of self-benefit to encompass the welfare of other people and society as a whole. In so doing, the pursuit of what one can do for oneself undergoes a pivotal shift to what ought to be done for the benefit of both oneself and others. As I see it, this shift in the central thrust of our lives is crucial. This is something that can be seen, for example, in the pioneering approaches to environmental issues adopted by the German people. I believe that if this way of life and behavior becomes firmly rooted in society, we will have built a basis for preventing the rebound effect from ever happening.

HAPPINESS ITSELF

WEIZSÄCKER: As part of this effort to expand outward the realm of self-benefit to include the welfare of others and society as a whole, I think it is important to strive to live in a sustainable society and to work in a company—including profit-making enterprises—that does not operate on the premise of destroying nature. These can become pillars supporting sustainability.

Of course, people are individuals, and living in a good social environment does not automatically mean we will avoid destruction and ethical failings. While the individual has a very important role to play, I still think that working for an ethically responsible company or enterprise is of great assistance in avoiding destructive attitudes.

I want to bring our dialogue to a close with one final point concerning teamwork between Europe and Asia. The majority of the great religions of the world recognizes and preaches that greed is bad and teaches a lifestyle reflecting that truth, standing in opposition to the market fundamentalism exhorting us that "greed is good." I have repeatedly stressed the importance of an alliance between Europeans and Asians, and I also urge such an alliance in the realms of ethics and religion.

Through such a political, economic, moral, and religious alliance, we can find the will and strength to stand against competition as the decisive criterion in all things, to stand against unchecked and inhumane market forces destroying the power of the state to protect the welfare of its citizens. And we can stand against the destruction of morals and the short-termism that many today seem to support and cherish, almost as a human right.

IKEDA: Your proposal carries much weight and worth.

A maxim popular in the 1930s and often attributed to Mahatma Gandhi reads, "Earth provides enough to satisfy every man's need but not every man's greed." The Earth does not have the capacity to sate limitless human greed. Continuing as we are now can only result in the present generation squandering the resources needed for future generations to survive.

It is a difficult problem, yet, as the saying goes, "The longest way round can be the shortest way home." I believe that to avert and ultimately resolve the predicament humankind faces, we need to revise our perception of happiness, which now equates mass consumption—the endless pursuit of desire—with fulfillment.

As I have said, Mahayana Buddhism teaches that earthly desires are the springboard to enlightenment. We must not allow ourselves to become captives of our desires but redirect the deep-seated energies of life underlying these base impulses toward the greater aims and values of harmonious coexistence and co-prosperity, toward building a better society, redirecting our way of life toward true fulfillment and happiness, or enlightenment.

I believe a core mission and responsibility of religion is to offer perspectives that will sustain us in the challenge of transforming the times. Such insights should enable us to reassess the plethora of materialistic values on which society places such a premium today and reorient every individual's life in a more positive direction.

I am deeply grateful to have had this opportunity to engage in a frank exchange of opinions with you, Dr. Weizsäcker, one of Europe's leading environmental scientists, and to have learned so much in the process. Thank you for all that you have contributed to our dialogue over the last several years. The SGI intends to continue to work together with you and the Club of Rome, forging stronger ties to advance toward our shared goal of building a society in which people can experience true satisfaction and happiness. Our goal is to contribute to a truly global transformation. This is our heartfelt hope.

APPENDIX 1

Selected Works
Daisaku Ikeda

A Forum for Peace: Daisaku Ikeda's Proposals to the UN. London: I.B. Tauris & Co. Ltd, 2014.

A New Humanism: The University Addresses of Daisaku Ikeda. London: I.B. Tauris & Co. Ltd, 2010.

A Quest for Global Peace with Joseph Rotblat. London: I.B. Tauris & Co. Ltd, 2007.

A Lifelong Quest for Peace with Linus Pauling. London: I.B. Tauris & Co. Ltd, 2009.

Before It's Too Late with Aurelio Peccei. London: I.B. Tauris & Co. Ltd, 2009.

Choose Life with Arnold Toynbee. London: I.B. Tauris & Co. Ltd, 2007.

Into Full Flower: Making Peace Cultures Happen with Elise Boulding. Cambridge, Mass.: Dialogue Path Press, 2010.

Our World To Make: Hinduism, Buddhism, and the Rise of Global Civil Society with Ved Nanda. Cambridge, Mass.: Dialogue Path Press, 2015.

Planetary Citizenship with Hazel Henderson. Santa Monica, Calif.: Middleway Press, 2004.

Selected Works
Ernst Ulrich von Weizsäcker

Earth Politics. London: Zed Books, 1994.

Ecological Tax Reform: Policy Proposal for Sustainable Development with Jochen Jesinghaus. London: Zed Books, 1992.

Factor Five: Transforming the Global Economy through 80% Improvememts in Resource Productivity with Charlie Hargroves. London, Earthscan, 2009.

Factor Four: Doubling Wealth—Halving Resource Use. A Report to the Club of Rome with Amory B. and L. Hunter Lovins, London: Earthscan, 1997.

Limits to Privatization—How to Avoid Too Much of A Good Thing with Oran Young and Matthias Finger. London, Earthscan, 2005.

New Frontiers in Technology Application: Integration of Emerging and Traditional Technologies with M. S. Swaminathan and Aklilu Lemma. Dublin, Oxford: Tycooly, 1983.

APPENDIX 3

The Göttingen Manifesto

The undersigned nuclear researchers are deeply concerned with the plans to equip the Bundeswehr with nuclear weapons. Some of us have raised our concerns a few months ago with the appropriate federal minister. Today the debate on this question has become general knowledge. The undersigned therefore feel the requirement to speak up about facts known to experts, but which seem to be inadequately known to the public.

1) Tactical nuclear weapons have the same destructive effect as normal atomic bombs. They are "tactical" only insofar as they are applied not only to civilian residences, but also to ground troops. Every single tactical nuclear weapon has a similar effect to the first atom bomb which destroyed Hiroshima. Since tactical nuclear weapons are available in significant numbers their destructive effect is on the whole much larger. They are only "small" in comparison to recently developed bombs, principally the hydrogen bomb.

2) There is no natural limit for the development of life-threatening effects of strategic nuclear weapons. Today a tactical nuclear weapon can destroy a small city, and a hydrogen bomb can render an entire region such as the Ruhr Valley uninhabitable. Already

today, one can probably wipe out the entire population of West Germany with the radioactivity from H-bombs. We know of no technical means to protect a large population from this threat.

We realise how difficult it is to foresee the political consequences of these facts. Since we are apolitical, no one expects us to do so. Our profession, i.e. pure science and its application, through which we bring many young people into our fold, leaves us with the responsibility for the potential effects of these actions. Therefore we cannot remain silent to all political issues. We align ourselves with the freedom that the Western world represents against Communism. We cannot deny the fear of the H-bomb contributes to the maintenance of peace in the whole world, and freedom in part of the world. However this form of peace and freedom is in the long term untenable, and the collapse of this situation is potentially deadly. We have no expertise to make concrete political suggestions to the Superpowers. We believe that a small country such as West Germany is best protected, and world peace most assisted, when nuclear weapons of any type are banned. In any case, none of the undersigned are prepared to participate in the creation, testing or deployment of any type of nuclear weapon. At the same time we feel it is extremely important that we continue to work together on the peaceful development of nuclear energy.

(Signed by Fritz Bopp, Max Born, Rudolf Fleischmann, Walther Gerlach, Otto Hahn, Otto Haxel, Werner Heisenberg, Hans Kopfermann, Max von Laue, Heinz Maier-Leibnitz, Josef Mattauch, Friedrich Paneth, Wolfgang Paul, Wolfgang Riezler, Fritz Strassmann, Wilhelm Walcher, Carl Friedrich von Weizsäcker, Karl Wirtz)

Notes

CONVERSATION ONE
HOPE AND RECOVERY

1. Tsunesaburo Makiguchi (1871–1944) was a forward-thinking educational theorist and religious reformer in Japan. His opposition to Japan's militarism and nationalism led to his imprisonment and death during World War II. Makiguchi is best known for two major works, *A Geography of Human Life* and *The System of Value-Creating Pedagogy*, and as founder, with Josei Toda in 1930, of the Soka Gakkai, which is today Japan's largest lay Buddhist organization. Consistent throughout his writing and in his work as a classroom teacher and school principal is his belief in the centrality of the happiness of the individual. This same commitment can be seen in his role as a religious reformer: He rejected the attempts of authorities to subvert the essence of the Buddhist teachings, insisting that religion exists to serve human needs.

2. The year 2011 marked the beginning of this dialogue between Dr. Ernst Ulrich von Weizsäcker and President Daisaku Ikeda, which was originally serialized in *Ushio*, a monthly Japanese literary magazine, and in the Japanese edition of *The Journal of Oriental Studies*, a biannual journal of the Institute of Oriental Philosophy, in eight installments from December 2011 to May 2014. The hardcover edition was published in Japanese by Ushio Publishing Company in October 2014 under the title *Chikyu kakumei e no chosen—ningen to*

kankyo o kataru (The Challenge of Global Transformation—Humanity and the Environment).

3. Makiguchi developed an approach to teaching geography that was intended to empower students with a dynamic and critical understanding of the world by grasping the relationship between geographic features and human activity. The 1903 publication of *A Geography of Human Life*—when Makiguchi was thirty-two—is considered one of his two most important publications. In it, Makiguchi rejected the prevailing approach to the study of geography, which was based on the rote memorization of facts and place names, and instead advocated a systematized, rational approach based on the relationship of nature and society to human life. The book consists of three major sections: 1) the land as the site of humanity's life activities; 2) nature as the medium for mutual interactions between humans and the land; and 3) the phenomena of humanity's life activities with Earth as their stage. *A Geography of Human Life* was reprinted numerous times.

4. Soka University and Soka Women's College, both located in Hachioji, Japan, are part of the Soka school system, which began in 1968 with the Soka Junior and Senior High Schools, established by Daisaku Ikeda in Kodaira, Tokyo. The system today includes elementary and other junior and senior high schools in Japan and a university in Aliso Viejo, California. Kindergartens have also been established in Hong Kong, Singapore, Malaysia, South Korea, and Brazil. Soka education is student driven and focuses on the happiness of the individual.

5. Starting in 1983, Daisaku Ikeda began composing peace proposals and sending them annually to the United Nations on January 26, SGI Day, the anniversary of the 1975 founding of the Soka Gakkai International. These proposals offer perspectives on critical issues facing humanity, suggesting solutions and responses grounded in Buddhist humanism. They also put forth specific agendas to strengthen the United Nations, including avenues for the involvement of civil society.

6. This magnitude 9.0 undersea earthquake, often referred to in Japan as the Great East Japan Earthquake, struck about 43 miles off Japan's eastern coast on Friday, March 11, 2011. It was the strongest earthquake known to have hit Japan, and the fifth most powerful in the world (since modern recordkeeping began in 1900). The earthquake

triggered powerful tsunamis as high as 130 feet, which travelled inland up to six miles in Japan's Tohoku and Sendai areas. There were reported to be 15,883 deaths and 2,667 missing throughout 22 prefectures.

7. The Soka Gakkai International, which includes organizations in 192 nations and territories around the world, has a long history of humanitarian relief efforts in response to earthquakes and other natural disasters. In addition to financial contributions to groups such as the Red Cross, the SGI (either directly or through an individual nation organization) has sent volunteers to assist in relief efforts, for example, following the devastation of Hurricane Katrina in Louisiana in 2005. In other cases, SGI community centers have provided shelter for people forced to evacuate their homes, for example, in the aftermath of the March 11, 2011, earthquake and tsunami in Japan. In another example, SGI-Chile members collected supplies to deliver to a relief center after that country's 2014 earthquake, and in 2015 in Malaysia, SGI members held a blood donation and organ pledge drive.

8. The March 11, 2011, earthquake and tsunami in Tohoku, Japan, caused equipment failures leading to the Fukushima Daiichi nuclear disaster (specifically, three nuclear meltdowns and the release of radioactive materials) beginning on March 12. It is considered the largest nuclear disaster since the 1986 Chernobyl disaster, and the second disaster (after Chernobyl) to be given the Level 7 event classification of the International Nuclear Event Scale, releasing an estimated 10 to 30 percent of the radiation of the Chernobyl accident.

9. Nichiren, *The Writings of Nichiren Daishonin*, vol. 1 (Tokyo: Soka Gakkai, 1999), p. 1119.

10. A few days after the March 2011 Fukushima nuclear disaster, large anti-nuclear protests were held through Germany. On May 29, 2011, Chancellor Angela Merkel announced that all Germany's nuclear power plants would close by 2022, much earlier than previously established. Eight of Germany's seventeen reactors were permanently shut down following the Fukushima accident.

11. Translated from Japanese. "Ondanka taisaku no kagi wa enerugi no koritsuka" (Efficient Energy Use Is the Key to Global Warming Solutions: An Interview with Ernst Ulrich von Weizsäcker), September 2010 *Ushio*, p. 88

12. Aurelio Peccei and Daisaku Ikeda, *Before It Is Too Late: A Dialogue* (London: I.B. Tauris, 2009), p. 18.

13. Ricardo Díez-Hochleitner and Daisaku Ikeda, *A Dialogue Between East and West: Looking to a Human Revolution* (London: I.B. Tauris, 2008), p. 1.

14. Dr. Weizsäcker was founding president of the Wuppertal Institute for Climate, Environment and Energy, headquartered in Germany, from 1991 to 2000.

15. *See* Daisaku Ikeda, "Dr. Aurelio Peccei, Cofounder of the Club of Rome," December 2000 *Living Buddhism*, p. 40.

16. Thomas Hobbes, *The English Works of Thomas Hobbes of Malmesbury*, vol. 2 (London: John Bohn Publisher, 1841), p. ii.

17. Ibid.

18. Robert B. Reich, *Supercapitalism: The Transformation of Business, Democracy, and Everyday Life* (New York: Alfred A. Knopf, 2007), p. 5.

19. Nichiren, *The Writings of Nichiren Daishonin*, vol. 1, p. 24.

CONVERSATION TWO
A WORLD WITHOUT WAR

1. Translated from German. Martin Wein, *Die Weizsäckers: Geschichte einer deutschen Familie* (The Weizsäckers: The Story of a German Family) (Stuttgart: Deutsche Verlags-Anstalt GmbH, 1988), p. 335.

2. Also known as the Mukden Incident. On September 18, 1931, a Japanese officer caused a small explosion close to a railway line owned by Japan's South Manchuria Railway near the town of Mukden (now Shenyang). The Imperial Japanese Army blamed Chinese dissidents for the explosion and proceeded to occupy Manchuria, establishing the puppet state of Manchukuo six months later. Japan's ruse was soon exposed to the international community, leading to Japan's diplomatic isolation and its March 1933 withdrawal from the League of Nations.

3. The Max Planck Society for the Advancement of Science was founded in 1948 and is an independent, nongovernmental, not-for-profit association of German research institutes (as of 2015, it comprises eighty-three institutes). Its primary goal is to support fundamental research in the nature, life, and social sciences; the arts; and humanities. It was named in honor of its former president, theoretical physicist Max Planck.

4. Max von Laue (1879–1960), Max Karl Ernst Ludwig Planck (1858–1947), Adolf Otto Reinhold Windaus (1876–1959), Werner Karl Heisenberg (1901–1976), and Max Born (1882–1970).

5. The Iron Curtain was a series of border defenses, the most famous of which was the Berlin Wall, which divided the city of Berlin. The Iron Curtain symbolized the ideological conflict cutting Europe into two separate areas, starting in 1945 at the end of World War II and lasting until the end of the Cold War in 1991. On the eastern side was the Soviet Union and its satellite states.

6. Otto Hahn (1879–1968) discovered nuclear fission and is often called the father of nuclear chemistry and the founder of the atomic age.

7. Werner Heisenberg (1901–76) was a theoretical physicist who made pioneering contributions to quantum mechanics and is best known for articulating, in 1927, the uncertainty principle, which states that the more precisely the position of some particle is determined, the less precisely its momentum can be known, and vice versa.

8. On July 26, 1956, Egyptian president Gamal Abdel Nasser nationalized the Suez Canal, which until then had been controlled by French and British interests. Britain and France anticipated that Nasser would block petroleum shipments through the Persian Gulf, so when diplomatic efforts to settle the crisis failed, they found an ally in Israel, whose military invaded Egypt and advanced toward the canal. By early November, British and French forces occupied the canal, but the United Nations soon evacuated all forces, and eventually Nasser emerged victorious. Britain and France consequently lost most of their influence in the Middle East.

9. The Hungarian Uprising, also known as the Hungarian Revolution of 1956: A spontaneous nationwide revolt against the government of the People's Republic of Hungary and its Soviet-imposed policies, October 23–November 10, 1956. It was the first major threat to Soviet control since the USSR's forces drove out the Nazis at the end of World War II and occupied Eastern Europe. Despite the failure of the uprising, it was highly influential and played a role in the downfall of the Soviet Union decades later.

10. Lutz Castell and Otfried Ischebeck, *Time, Quantum and Information* (New York: Springer Science & Business Media, April 17, 2013), p. 51.

11. Ibid.

12. On July 9, 1955, in the midst of the Cold War, the Russell-Einstein

Manifesto—considered one of the most influential statements about the threat of nuclear weapons—was issued. Initiated by mathematician and philosopher Bertrand Russell and world-renowned scientist Albert Einstein, it was signed by a total of eleven leading scientists and intellectuals. The document outlined the dangers posed by nuclear weapons and called for world leaders to seek peaceful resolutions to conflict. A few days after its release, philanthropist Cyrus S. Eaton offered to sponsor a conference (as called for in the manifesto) in Pugwash, Nova Scotia (Eaton's birthplace). This conference, held in July 1957, became the first of the Pugwash Conferences on Science and World Affairs. Einstein signed the document a few days before his death on April 18, 1955.

13. Second Soka Gakkai president Josei Toda made his historic declaration calling for the abolition of nuclear weapons on September 8, 1957, at a meeting of 50,000 members of the Soka Gakkai's youth division at Mitsuzawa Stadium in Yokohama, Japan. His stance was that nuclear weapons and their use must be absolutely condemned, not from the standpoint of ideology, nationality, or ethnic identity but from the universal dimension of humanity and our inalienable right to live.

14. Joseph Rotblat and Daisaku Ikeda, *A Quest for Global Peace: Rotblat and Ikeda on War, Ethics and the Nuclear Threat* (London: I.B. Tauris, 2007), p. 5.

15. Translated from Japanese. Georg Picht, *Ima koko de* (*Hier und Jetzt: Philosophieren nach Auschwitz und Hiroshima* [Here and Now: Philosophizing after Auschwitz and Hiroshima]), trans. Ryoji Asano (Tokyo: Hosei University Press, 1986), p. 5.

16. Translated from Japanese. Carl Friedrich von Weizsäcker, *Wareware wa doko e iku noka* (*Wohin gehen wir?* [Where Are We Going?]), trans. Katsuji Kosugi (Kyoto: Minerva Shobo, 2004), p. 29.

17. Translated from Japanese. Tsuneaki Kato, *Vaitsuzekka* (Weizsäcker), Series: Century Books, *Hito to shiso* (Person and Thought), 111, p. 59.

18. Willy Brandt was the fourth chancellor of the Federal Republic of Germany (West Germany) from 1969 to 1974. He implemented policies aimed at normalizing relations with Eastern Europe, especially the German Democratic Republic (East Germany). Termed *Ostpolitik* (New Eastern Policy), this effort to bring change through rapproche-

ment is credited by some with leading to the opening of the Berlin Wall in 1989 and its collapse in 1990.

19. Clash of Civilizations: The theory that people's cultural and religious identities will be the primary source of conflict in the post-Cold War period.

20. Carl Friedrich von Weizsäcker, *Carl Friedrich von Weizsäcker: Major Texts on Politics and Peace Research*, SpringerBriefs on Pioneers in Science and Practice, vol. 25, ed. Ulrich Bartosch (New York: Springer, 2015), pp. 60–61.

21. Translated from Japanese. Carl Friedrich von Weizsäcker, *Wareware wa doko e iku noka*, p. ii.

22. The Biological Weapons Convention was the first multilateral disarmament treaty banning the development, production, and stockpiling of an entire category of weapons of mass destruction. It was opened for signature on April 10, 1972, and entered into force on March 26, 1975.

23. People's Decade for Nuclear Abolition, "Interview with Jayantha Dhanapala on SGI President Ikeda's Peace Proposal," March 15, 2011 (accessed at <http://www.peoplesdecade.org/news/experts/detail.php?id=157> on February 21, 2015).

24. Translated from Japanese. Carl Friedrich von Weizsäcker, *Kokoro no yamai to shite no heiwa fuzai (Der ungesicherte friede* [The Insecure Peace]) (Tokyo: Nanun-do, 1982), p. 193.

Conversation Three
Green Growth

1. Nichiren, *The Writings of Nichiren Daishonin*, vol. 1, p. 621.

2. For the 2012 Rio+20, the SGI organized its sustainable development exhibition *Seeds of Hope*, which was created jointly with Earth Charter International, and also cohosted a roundtable discussion on education titled "The Future We Create." In addition, President Ikeda submitted a new environmental proposal, "For a Sustainable Global Society: Learning for Empowerment and Leadership."

3. Human Development Report 2007/2008 (accessed at <http://hdr .undp.org/en/media/HDR_20072008_Summary_English.pdf> on September 2, 2011).

4. In 1998, Japan initiated the Top Runner Program to improve energy efficiency of end-use products and to develop leading edge energy-efficient products. By 2009, the program had achieved mandatory energy efficiency standards for twenty-one products. It is now considered one of the major pillars of Japanese climate policy.

5. *See* Hazel Henderson, Daisaku Ikeda, *Planetary Citizenship* (Santa Monica, Calif.: Middleway Press, 2004).

6. Translated from Japanese. Hazel Henderson, "Shikishaga kataru: Jidai o hiraku chikara ga koko ni" (Scholarly Talk: Power to Open a New Age), March 27, 2011, *Seikyo Shimbun*.

7. Changing poison to medicine: The principle that earthly desires and suffering can be transformed into benefit and enlightenment by virtue of the power of the Law of Nam-myoho-renge-kyo.

8. The Calvert-Henderson Quality of Life Indicators measure conditions and trends in twelve key socioeconomic sectors of the United States, as identified and defined by independent futurist and economist Hazel Henderson and the Calvert Group, Inc., headquartered in Bethesda, Md. These indicators include: education, employment, energy, environment, health, human rights, income, infrastructure, national security, public safety, recreation, and shelter. For more information, *see* < http://hazelhenderson.com/2002/01/06/a-systems-approach-calvert-henderson-quality-of-life-indicators/ > (accessed on September 29, 2015).

9. Global casino: Often used to describe stock markets. More broadly, it is the situation in which enormous assets are traded daily for speculative profits in global financial markets rather than for the benefit of the economy (accessed at < http://hazelhenderson.com/1998/10/30/rules-to-tame-the-global-casino-october-1998/ > on November 27, 2015).

10. Federal Ministry for the Environment, Nature Conservation and Nuclear Safety, "Speech delivered by Federal Chancellor Angela Merkel at the Second Petersberg Climate Dialogue" (accessed at < http://www.bmu.de/english/petersberg_conference/doc/47612. php> on September 14, 2011).

11. The April 26, 1986, disaster at the Chernobyl nuclear power plant in Ukraine was the result of a flawed Soviet reactor design coupled with operator errors. The resulting steam explosion and fires released at least 5 percent of the radioactive reactor core into the atmosphere. Thirty people died within three months as a result of acute radiation

poisoning. As of 2008, there have been sixty-four confirmed deaths. This disaster led to major changes in safety culture and in industry cooperation, particularly between East and West before the end of the Soviet Union.

12. Translated from Japanese. *Kankyo bijinesu* (Environmental Business Online), "Creation of IRENA—The Key to Energy Security and the Reduction of CO2: An Interview with Hermann Scheer," March 6, 2009 (accessed at <http://www.kankyo-business.jp/news/003528.php> on September 14, 2011).

13. *The Writings of Thomas Jefferson: Being His Autobiography, Correspondence, Reports, Messages, Addresses, and Other Writings, Official and Private,* vol. 6 (New York: J. C. Riker, 1857), p. 180.

14. Translated from Japanese. *Kankyo Bijinesu,* op. cit.

15. The mission of the DESERTEC Foundation is the worldwide implementation of solutions to provide climate protection, energy security, and development by generating sustainable power from the sites where renewable sources of energy are at their most abundant. For more information, go to <http://www.desertec.org/en/> (accessed on September 30, 2015).

16. *See* "Club of Rome Pursues Human Security," December 26, 2003, *World Tribune,* p. 1. Also appears in Japanese: October 17, 2003, *Seikyo Shimbun.*

17. Translated from Japanese. "Jinrui no unmei wa seinen no kyoiku ni" (Fate of Humanity Depends on Education of Youth), December 26, 2002, *Seikyo Shimbun.*

18. Ernst von Weizsäcker, Karlson "Charlie" Hargroves, Michael H. Smith, Cheryl Desha, Peter Stasinopoulos, *Factor Five: Transforming the Global Economy through 80% Improvements in Resource Productivity* (London: Earthscan, 2009), p. 343.

19. *See* ibid., pp. 342–343.

20. The Earth Charter is intended to be an ethical framework for a just, sustainable, and peaceful global society in the 21st century. It began as a United Nations initiative and developed through a decade-long, worldwide, cross-cultural dialogue on shared goals and values involving more than 6,000 organizations, including the SGI, that was finalized on June 29, 2000. The Earth Charter is acquiring soft law status, considered to be morally, but not legally, binding on governments that endorse them. Together with the Earth Charter Initiative, the SGI created an exhibition titled *Seeds of Change: The Earth Charter*

and Human Potential, that was viewed in 13 languages and 26 countries by more than 1.5 million people. In 2010, on the 10th anniversary of the Earth Charter, the exhibition was revised as *Seeds of Hope: Visions of Sustainability, Steps toward Change* and has been shown in 20 countries.

CONVERSATION FOUR
SUFFICIENCY AND HUMAN FULFILLMENT

1. Weizsäcker, et al., *Factor Five*, pp. 349–350.
2. Ibid., p. 350.
3. Ernst Ulrich von Weizsäcker, *Earth Politics* (London: Zed Books Ltd., 1994), p. 113.
4. Green Climate Fund: A fund within the UN Framework Convention on Climate Change intended to assist developing countries in practices countering climate change.
5. In 1995, the German Advisory Council on Global Change (WBGU) suggested that global warming should be limited to a maximum of 2°C above the preindustrial level in order to prevent interference with the climate system. In the December 2009 Copenhagen Accord, many countries agreed and have made 2°C an official goal. A flat distribution (the budget approach) of emissions rights among all people based on "one human—one emissions entitlement" (the "per capita equal emission rights approach") is aimed at including developing countries. In fact, countries with below-average per capita emissions can sell surplus emissions rights to countries with higher per capita emissions.
6. Translated from Japanese. *See* Tokuji Maruyama, "Kogai seigi" (Pollution and Justice) in *Kankyo rinrigaku* (Environmental Ethics), eds. Shuichi Kito and Mayumi Fukunaga (Tokyo: University of Tokyo Press, 2009), p. 71.
7. "Kenpo ni kankyoken no kitei o" (The Establishment of a Right to a Healthy Environment in the Constitution), August 19, 2002, *Mainichi Shimbun*.
8. *See Environmental Policy in Japan*, eds. Shigeto Tsuru and Helmut Weidner (Berlin: Edition Sigma Rainer Bohn Verlag, 1989).
9. These four diseases are considered the "four big pollution diseases" (*yondai kogai-byo*) of Japan. Although Itai-itai disease first broke

out in 1912, the rest all appeared in the 1950s and 1960s, leading to comprehensive environmental policies and, in 1971, the creation of Japan's Environmental Agency.

10. Johann Wolfgang von Goethe, Johann Peter Eckermann, and Frederic Jacob Soret, *Conversations of Goethe with Eckermann and Soret* (London: Smith, Elder & Co., 65, 1850), p. 420.

11. James Simpson, *Matthew Arnold and Goethe* (London: The Modern Humanities Research Association, 1979), p. 151.

12. "People's Decade for Nuclear Abolition, Commentary by Tibor Tóth on the SGI President's Peace Proposal" (accessed at <http://www.peoplesdecade.org/news/experts/detail.php?id=154> on September 15, 2011).

13. Weizsäcker, et al., *Factor Five*, p. 320.

14. Translated from Japanese. Hans Henningsen and Daisaku Ikeda, *Asu o tsukuru kyoiku no seigyo* (Shaping the Future: The Sacred Task of Education) (Tokyo: Ushio Publishing Co., Ltd., 2009), p. 295.

15. Ibid., p. 296.

16. Human Development Report 2007/2008 (accessed at <http://hdr.undp.org/en/media/HDR_20072008_EN_Complete.pdf> on October 15, 2011).

17. Nichiren, *The Writings of Nichiren Daishonin*, vol. 1, p. 1120.

18. Rotblat and Ikeda, *A Quest for Global Peace*, p. 91.

19. Linus Pauling and Daisaku Ikeda, *A Lifelong Quest for Peace* (London: I.B. Tauris, 2009), p. 37.

20. Friedrich Wilhelm Christian Karl Ferdinand von Humboldt (1767–1835): Prussian philosopher, government functionary, diplomat, and founder of Humboldt University of Berlin.

CONVERSATION FIVE
THE LONG-TERM PERSPECTIVE

1. Donella H. Meadows, Dennis L. Meadows, Jørgen Randers, and William W. Behrens III, *The Limits to Growth* (New York: Universe Books, 1974), p. 184.

2. Lester R. Brown, *World on the Edge: How to Prevent Environmental and Economic Collapse* (New York: W. W. Norton & Co., 2011), p. 137.

3. Ibid., pp. 6, 37.

4. *See* Daisaku Ikeda, "For a Sustainable Global Society: Learning for

Empowerment and Leadership" (environment proposal, June 5, 2012) (accessed at <http://www.sgi.org/assets/pdf/environmentpro-posal2012.pdf> on November 27, 2015).

5. Michelle Bachelet served as executive director of UN Women from March 2010 to September 2013, when she resigned to prepare for her second term as president of Chile.

6. Translated from Japanese. Co-chair Puntenney's statement appears in the June 26, 2012, *Seikyo Shimbun*.

7. The Brazil SGI Amazon Ecological Conservation Center was founded in 1992 (at the time of the Rio Earth Summit) in the suburbs of Manaus, Brazil.

8. *The Lotus Sutra and Its Opening and Closing Sutras*, trans. Burton Watson (Tokyo: Soka Gakkai, 2009), p. 272.

9. *See* Daisaku Ikeda, "Human Security and Sustainability: Sharing Reverence for the Dignity of Life" (2012 peace proposal) in *A Forum for Peace*, ed. Olivier Urbain (New York: I.B. Tauris, 2014), pp. 471–513.

10. *See* Michael C. Graffagna and Yoshinobu Mizutani, "Outline of Japan's Feed-In Tariff Law for Renewable Electric Energy," 2011 (accessed at <http://media.mofo.com/files/Uploads/Images/110913-Outline-of-Japans-Feed-In-Tariff-Law-for-Renewable-Electric-Energy.pdf> on January 5, 2015).

11. Translated from Japanese. Dr. Weizsäcker's speech appears in the April 2, 2012, *Tokyo Shimbun*.

12. Just-in-time production, also known as the Toyota production system, aims to reduce flow times in production schedules (including response times from suppliers and to customers). It started in Japan in the 1960s and 1970s and migrated to Western industries in the 1980s.

CONVERSATION SIX
ENVIRONMENTAL AWARENESS

1. *The Sutta-Nipāta*, trans. H. Saddhatissa (London: Curzon Press, 1985), p. 16.

2. As of July 2014, the Kansai students have participated forty-five times, the highest participation in the world.

3. Translated from German. German Embassy, *Kankyo senshinkoku doitsu* (Advanced Environmental Nation Germany) (accessed at

< http://www.eureka.tu.chiba-u.ac.jp/study/enen/germany/germany .pdf > on February 24, 2015).

4. Currently available only in German.

5. Translated from German. Dietrich Jörn Weder, *Umwelt: Bedrohung und Bewahrung* (Environment: Threats and Conservation) (Bonn: Bundeszentrale für politische Bildung, 2003), p. 5.

6. Translated from Japanese. Anwarul K. Chowdhury and Daisaku Ikeda, *Atarashiki chikyu shakai no sozo e—heiwa no bunka to kokuren o kataru* (Creating a New Global Society—A Discourse on the United Nations and a Culture of Peace) (Tokyo: Ushio Publishing Co., Ltd., 2011), pp. 418–419.

7. Translated from Japanese. Johann Wolfgang von Goethe, *Gete kaku-gen-shu* (Words of Wisdom of Goethe) (Tokyo: Shinchosha Publishing Co., Ltd., 1982), p. 89.

8. *See* WWF, *Living Planet Report 2012*, p. 12 (accessed at < http://awsas-sets.panda.org/downloads/1_lpr_2012_online_full_size_single_pages_final_120516.pdf > on November 27, 2015).

9. Ibid.

10. Ibid.

11. *See* Eisuke Ishikawa, *Oedo risaikuru jijo* (Recycling System in Great Edo) (Tokyo: Kodansha, 1994), pp. 24, 32, 60, 265, 266, 273.

CONVERSATION SEVEN
SOCIAL AND ECOLOGICAL JUSTICE

1. *See* UNEP, "High Level Panel Releases Recommendations for World's Next Development Agenda" (accessed at < http://www.unep.org/newscentre/default.aspx?DocumentID=2716&ArticleID=9516 > on August 7, 2013).

2. *See* European Commission, "A Decent Life for All: Ending poverty and giving the world a sustainable future," Brussels, 27.2.201, COM(2013) 92 final.

3. *See* Daisaku Ikeda, "Compassion, Wisdom and Courage: Building a Global Society of Peace and Creative Coexistence" (2013 peace proposal) in *A Forum for Peace*, pp. 515–552.

4. Ernst Ulrich von Weizsäcker, *Earth Politics*, p. 211.

5. *See* Ministry of Agriculture, Forestry and Fisheries of Japan (accessed at < http://www.maff.go.jp/j/shokusan/recycle/syoku_loss/

pdf/0902shokurosu.pdf> on January 10, 2014).

6. Ibid.

7. *See* Katsumi Hirano, *Keizai tairiku afurika* (Economic Continent: Africa) (Tokyo: Chuokoron-Shinsha, Inc., 2013), pp. 140–141.

8. Ernst Friedrich Schumacher, *Small Is Beautiful: A Study of Economics as if People Mattered* (London: Blond & Briggs Ltd., 1973), pp. 103–104.

9. *See* Ikeda, "Compassion, Wisdom and Courage" in *A Forum for Peace*, pp. 515–552.

10. Schumacher, *Small Is Beautiful*, p. 107.

11. Nichiren, *The Writings of Nichiren Daishonin*, vol. 2 (Tokyo: Soka Gakkai, 2006), p. 842.

12. Ibid., vol. 1, p. 644.

13. Ibid.

14. UNDP, "Beyond Scarcity: Power, Poverty and the Global Water Crisis" (accessed at <http://hdr.undp.org/sites/default/files/reports/267/hdr06-complete.pdf> on August 7, 2013).

15. Ibid.

16. *See* "The Millennium Development Goals Report 2012" (accessed at <http://www.un.org/millenniumgoals/pdf/MDG%20Report%20 2012.pdf> on August 7, 2013).

17. Translated from German. Ernst U. von Weizsäcker, Karlson Hargroves, and Michael Smith, *Faktor Funf: Die Formel fur nachhaltiges Wachstum* (Factor Five: The Formula for Sustainable Growth) (Munich: Droemer, 2010), p. 334.

18. Catholic social teaching: The doctrine developed by the Catholic Church and addressing issues of social justice, poverty and wealth, economics, and the role of government. Its foundation is widely considered to have been laid by Pope Leo XIII's 1891 letter *Rerum novarum*, which advocated economic distributism.

19. "SGI kaicho Vaitsuzekka daitoryo to hirakareta shakai o kataru" (Open Society: A Discussion with SGI President Ikeda and Richard von Weizsäcker, the First President of Unified Germany), June 14, 1991, *Seikyo Shimbun*.

20. Ibid.

21. Translated from Japanese. *See* Richard von Weizsäcker, *Vaitsuzekka nihon koenroku: Rekishi ni me o tozasu na* (Richard von Weizsäcker's Lectures in Japan: We Must Not Shun the Lessons of History) (Tokyo: Iwanami Shoten, 1996), pp. 130–131.

22. Henderson, Ikeda, *Planetary Citizenship*, p. 156.

23. Ernst Ulrich von Weizsäcker, *Earth Politics*, p. 198.

24. *See* The Centre for Bhutan Studies, "An extensive analysis of GNH Index" (accessed at <http://www.grossnationalhappiness.com/wp-content/uploads/2012/10/An%20Extensive%20Analysis%20of%20GNH%20Index.pdf> on August 7, 2013).

25. Ibid.

26. *See* Genichi Yamazaki, *Ashoka-o to sono jidai* (The Time of King Ashoka) (Tokyo: Shunjyusha Publishing Company, 1982), pp. 182–183.

27. Ibid.

28. Ernst Ulrich von Weizsäcker, *Earth Politics*, p. 197.

29. Ibid., p. 199.

30. Ibid., p. 201.

31. *The Sutta-Nipāta*, trans. H. Saddhatissa, p. 16.

32. Nichiren, *The Record of the Orally Transmitted Teachings* (Tokyo: Soka Gakkai, 2004), p. 146.

33. Ibid.

34. Ernst von Weizsäcker, Amory B. Lovins, and L. Hunter Lovins, *Factor Four: Doubling Wealth, Halving Resource Use* (London: Earthscan, 1998), p. 295.

35. David Cayley, *Ivan Illich in Conversation* (Toronto: Anansi, 1992), p. 155.

36. Ibid., p. 157.

37. Schumacher, *Small Is Beautiful*, p. 68.

38. Weizsäcker, et al., *Factor Four*, p. 295.

39. Arnold Toynbee and Kei Wakaizumi, *Surviving the Future* (London: Oxford University Press, 1971), p. 89.

40. Translated from Japanese. *See* Arnold Toynbee, *Nihon no katsuro* (A Way Forward for Japan) (Tokyo: PHP Institute, Inc., 1974), p. 162.

CONVERSATION EIGHT
OUR SUSTAINABLE FUTURE

1. World Meteorological Association, press release no. 976, "The Global Climate 2001–2010" (accessed at <http://www.wmo.int/pages/mediacentre/press_releases/pr_976_en.html> on September 19, 2013).

2. Ibid.
3. *See* German Federal Foreign Office (accessed at < http://www.
   auswaertiges-amt.de/EN/Aussenpolitik/Friedenspolitik/Vereinte-
   Nationen/Schwerpunkte/VN-Klima-Kyoto.html> on February 25,
   2015).
4. National Aeronautics and Space Administration report (accessed at
   < http://www.nasa.gov/topics/earth/features/greenland-melt.html>
   on November 27, 2015).
5. Around August 18, 2010, NASA satellite imagery showed that a
   large parcel of ice, approximately the size of Bermuda, fractured
   from a massive ice shelf on Ellesmere Island in northeastern Canada (accessed at < http://www.cbc.ca/news/canada/north/huge-ice-
   chunk-breaks-off-ellesmere-island-1.973944> on November 27,
   2015).
6. United Nations Development Programme, "Human Development
   Report 2011" (accessed at < http://hdr.undp.org/sites/default/files/
   reports/271/hdr_2011_en_complete.pdf> on March 14, 2014).
7. In 1984, Freiburg's Environmental Card was introduced for 38 DM
   (US$13 at the time) for unlimited travel with the urban network. In
   1991, it was replaced by the RegioCard, costing 47 euros (US$61) a
   month.
8. M. S. Swaminathan and Daisaku Ikeda, *Revolutions: to green the
   environment, to grow the human heart* (New Delhi: EastWest Books
   [Madras] Pvt. Ltd., 2005), p. 69.
9. *The Dhammapada,* trans. Eknath Easwaran (London: Penguin Books,
   1986), p. 133.
10. *The Book of the Kindred Sayings (Saṃyutta-Nikāya),* trans. Rhys Davids
    (Oxford: The Pali Text Society, 1996), p. 146.
11. *The Sutta-Nipāta,* trans. H. Saddhatissa, p. 91.
12. *See* Nichiren, *The Record of the Orally Transmitted Teachings,* p. 11.
13. Aurelio Peccei, *The Human Quality* (Oxford: Pergamon Press, 1977),
    p. 13.

Index

About the Authors

ERNST ULRICH VON WEIZSÄCKER is former dean of the Donald Bren School of Environmental Science and Management at the University of California, Santa Barbara, and currently co-president of the Club of Rome. He studied chemistry and physics in Hamburg and graduated from the University of Freiburg in 1968. During the 1970s he was president of the University in Kassel before taking up the post of Director of the UN Centre for Science and Technology in New York. From 1984 to 1991 he was the Director of the Institute for European Environment Politics in Bonn, Paris and London and from 1991 to 2000 Dr. von Weizsäcker was the President of the Institute for Climate, Environment and Energy in Wuppertal, Germany. From 1998 to 2005 he was a member of the German Parliament. Prof. von Weizsäcker is the author or co-author of many books and publications, including *Earth Politics* (1994), *Factor Four: Doubling Wealth, Halving Resource Use* (1995), *Factor Five: Transforming the Global Economy through 80% Improvements in Resource Productivity* (2009). He was honored with the Takeda Award for World/Environmental Well-Being in 2001.

DAISAKU IKEDA is president of the Soka Gakkai International, a lay Buddhist organization with more than twelve million members worldwide. He has written and lectured widely on Buddhism, humanism, and global ethics. More than 70 of his dialogues have been published, including conversations with figures such as Mikhail Gorbachev, Hazel Henderson, Elise Boulding, Joseph Rotblat, Linus Pauling, and Arnold Toynbee. Dedicated to education that promotes humanistic ideals, Mr. Ikeda founded Soka University in Tokyo in 1971 and, in 2001, Soka University of America in Aliso Viejo, California. In furtherance of his vision of fostering dialogue and solidarity for peace, Mr. Ikeda has founded three independent, nonprofit research institutes: the Ikeda Center for Peace, Learning, and Dialogue, the Toda Institute for Global Peace and Policy Research, and the Institute of Oriental Philosophy.